# The Anglican Communion
# and Scripture

# The Anglican Communion and Scripture

## Papers from the First International Consultation of the Evangelical Fellowship in the Anglican Communion, Canterbury, UK, June 1993

**John Stott and Others**

regnum

THE EVANGELICAL FELLOWSHIP
IN THE ANGLICAN COMMUNION

First published 1996 by Regnum Books International and EFAC in association
with Paternoster Publishing, P.O. Box 300, Carlisle, Cumbria CA3 0QS UK

Regnum Books International

P.O. Box 70, Oxford, OX2 6HB, UK

17951 Cowan, Irvine, California, USA

P.O. Box 76, Akropong-Akuapem, Ghana

Jose Marmol 1734, 1602 Florida, Buenos Aires, Argentina

Post Bag No. 21, Vasant Kunj, New Dehli 110057, India

02 01 00 99 98 97 96      7 6 5 4 3 2 1

**British Library Cataloguing in Publication Data**

A catalogue record for this book is available from the British Library.

ISBN 1–870345–22–3

The Evangelical Fellowship in the Anglican Communion was founded in
1961 to foster fellowship among Anglican Evangelicals throughout the
world. It comprises of 19 national fellowships.

Regnum Books publishes on behalf of the African Theological Fraternity,
the Latin American Theological Fraternity, and Partnership in Mission in
Asia. It works in co-operation with major western Christian organisations
and is based at the Oxford Centre for Mission Studies,
P.O. Box 70, Oxford OX2 6HB, U.K.

Laserset in India by Wordmarkers
Printed and bound in Great Britain by
Clays Ltd, St Ives plc

# Contents

# Contributors

**Rev Dr John Stott** (UK) is Rector Emeritus of All Soul's Langham Place, London, founder Secretary (1961-1983) and sometime President (1986-1990) of the Evangelical Fellowship in the Anglican Communion (EFAC).

**Canon Dr Vinay Samuel** (India) is Executive Director of the International Fellowship of Evangelical Mission Theologians and of the Oxford Centre for Mission Studies. He was Secretary of EFAC (1986-88).

**Rev Dr Cyril Okorocha** (Nigeria) is Secretary for Evangelism of the Anglican Consultative Council.

**The Rt Rev Dr Michael Nazir Ali** (Pakistan) is Bishop of Rochester, former Bishop of Raiwind (Pakistan) (1984-1986), and General Secretary of the Church Missionary Society (1989-1994).

**Margaret Rodgers** (Australia) is the Research Officer of the General Synod Office of the Anglican Church of Australia and a President of the Christian Conference of Asia.

**Elaine Storkey** (UK) is Director of the Institute for Contemporary Christianity and an author and broadcaster. She is a member of the General Synod of the Church of England.

**Rev Dr Jesudasan Jeyaraj** (India) is Lecturer at the Tamilnadu Theological Seminary, Madurai, India.

**Rev Dr Christopher Wright** (UK) is Principal of All Nations Christian College, UK and co-ordinator of the Theological Resource Network of EFAC and formerly Lecturer at Union Biblical Seminary, Pune, India.

**The Rt Rev Mdimi Mhogolo** (Tanzania) is Bishop of the Diocese of Central Tanganyika, Tanzania and former Principal of St Philip's Theological College, Kongwa.

**Canon Graham Kings** (UK) is Henry Martyn Lecturer in Mission in the Cambridge Federation of Theological Colleges and former Lecturer at St. Andrew's College, Kabare, Kenya.

**The Rt Rev Dr Philip Le Feuvre** (South Africa) is Bishop of the Diocese of St Mark the Evangelist, Pietersburg, in the Northern Province of

South Africa. He was formerly Director of Studies at St. Paul's Theological College, Grahamstown and has been visiting Professor at Fuller Theological Seminary, USA.

**Rev Patrick Benson** (UK) is Vicar of Barnston, Merseyside, former Curate of St Mary's Upton and former Principal of St Andrew's College, Kabare, Kenya.

**Dr Ida Glaser** (UK) is Other Faiths Secretary for Crosslinks UK.

**Canon Peter C Moore** (Canada) is President of Trinity Episcopal School for Ministry, Ambridge, USA and formerly Rector of Little Trinity Church, Toronto and North American Regional Secretary of EFAC.

**Rev Alfredo Cooper** is a missionary with the South American Missionary Society. He is Pastor of Las Condes Church, Santiago and Diocesan and Provincial Evangelist.

# Preface

A recent survey of the Anglican Communion has shown that the average Anglican is aged between twenty and thirty, is brown-skinned, poor, lives in the Two-thirds world, and is evangelical. Evangelical people are Bible people. If the average Anglican is a Two-thirds World Evangelical, then evangelical perspectives on scripture should contribute significantly to mainstream Anglican thought. This book is a contribution to that process.

Further, an understanding of how Evangelicals use scripture is important for understanding Christian witness in those provinces of the Anglican Communion where the church is growing amidst poverty and religious pluralism. Such an understanding is also vital for Christian witness in the west, since while the Bible is an authority that talks about morality, western culture accepts neither authority nor morality. In such a situation the Church must challenge the modern world to enter the world of the Bible, and must place the culture of modernism in the spotlight of the Bible.

This book first places the Bible in the spotlight. What is meant by "verbal inspiration"? What links the Holy Spirit and the Holy Bible? Is there a particularly Anglican view of scripture to contribute to the ecumenical debate? Then it places cultures in the spotlight of the Bible. How does scripture inform the witness of the exploding Church in Tanzania and of a struggling congregation in a religiously plural inner-city in the UK? Can a Toronto church use the Bible to address the issue of homosexuality? How does a bishop use scripture to reform the structure of his diocese in South Africa or to address national injustice in Kenya?

These commitments and questions were addressed at the Canterbury Consultation of the Evangelical Fellowship in the

Anglican Communion in June 1993. This was the first international consultation in the history of EFAC. It brought together the leaders of the various national fellowships in each region and country together with those evangelicals in senior leadership where the majority expression of the Anglican Church is evangelical, for example in Kenya. These groups include EFAC Nigeria, Barnabas Ministries in Canada, the Latimer Fellowship in New Zealand, EFAC Australia, the Church of the Province of Kenya, the Fellowship of Witness in the United States, and the Church of England Evangelical Council in the United Kingdom. Subsequent to the consultation, similar gatherings have taken place such as Essentials 94, held in June 1994 in Montreal, Canada. Its proceedings were edited by George Egerton and published in Toronto in 1995 by Anglican Book Centre under the title *Anglican Essentials: Reclaiming Faith within the Anglican Church of Canada.* A further meeting of EFAC is planned to take place in Australia, 26-30 June 1996.

The purpose of the consultation was "to commend and strengthen biblical authority in the life and mission of the Church." Each day began and ended with worship, led by teams from the different cultures represented, following the order of service and music of their own lands. The consultation generated *The Canterbury Rap* which is reproduced here. Within the context of worship six Bible expositions were given on The Anglican Communion and Scripture. These were followed by theological papers on Scripture and Mission, Scripture and Ecumenical Dialogue, and Scripture and Social and Personal Morality. Each topic was then thoroughly addressed in discussion groups which contributed their findings to a Summary Findings Report. This concluded "The Church must challenge the modern world to enter the world of the Bible, and must place the culture of modernism in the spotlight of the Bible." This report was hailed by the (English) *Church Times* as "a ringing statement of mainstream Anglican evangelical attitudes to the Bible."

As part of the consultation the Theological Resource Network of EFAC engaged in theological reflection on case studies on the use of scripture in mission. The case studies and the reflections emerging from them are reproduced here. The TRN has previously contributed material on The Decade of Evangelism, published as *One Gospel, Many Clothes* (ed. Chris Wright and Chris Sugden, Regnum, 1989), on Inter-Faith Dialogue and Urban Mission. The Theological Network has met subsequently in South Africa (September 1995) to consider Church and State. Further consultations are being planned in the preparation for Lambeth 1998 in South Asia and the Caribbean and Latin America, focusing on a Theology of Humanity.

In addition to support from participants themselves, the Consultation was also supported by grants from the Lutheran Church of Wuerrtemburg in Germany, Fieldstead and Company in the USA and the Langham Trust. The publication of this book has been supported by the congregation of Little Trinity Church, Toronto, Canada. Details of the ongoing work of EFAC can be obtained through its annual publication, the *EFAC Bulletin*, available from the Oxford Centre for Mission Studies, P O Box 70, Oxford OX2 6HB, UK.

Oxford, Advent 1995　　　　　　**Christopher Sugden**
　　　　　　　　　　　　　　　Publications Secretary

# PART I
# BIBLICAL STUDIES

# Scripture in the Life of the Church

## SUMMARY FINDINGS REPORT

We met as 150 Evangelical Anglicans from 29 countries at Rutherford College at the University of Kent at Canterbury from June 28 to July 3 1993. We gathered to consult on "The Anglican Communion and Scripture." We studied the Bible's own teaching on the nature and authority of the Bible. We considered:

- Scripture, Mission and Evangelism;
- Scripture and Social and Personal Morality; and
- Scripture in Ecumenical Dialogue

We heard the witness of Christians in Africa, the Americas, Asia, Australasia and Europe. We received case studies on the use of Scripture, discussed co-operation in Mission and reflected on issues of Church and Nation. The following summarizes our main findings:

### A. The Nature of the Bible

The Bible is centred on the revelation of God in Christ. It discloses human sin, and God's judgment; but it also reveals the salvation which Christ won when he was crucified and raised from the dead. The Bible brings that revelation to human beings so that we may experience the love, grace and mercy of God. The whole of Scripture is to be first understood in the light of that central theme.

### *The Bible's double origin*

According to the Bible's own witness it is a divine word because, as Jesus promised, the Holy Spirit took what he had heard from the Father and the Son, and disclosed it to its writers. The Bible also testifies that it is a human book. Since it is the Word of God we read it humbly, in submission, as we read no other book. Because it is the words of human beings we also read it thoughtfully, intelligently, as we do any other book.

In our day the divine authorship and our proper response is often ignored or slighted. For example, the Bible's authority is undermined if the Church ignores part of the canon of Scripture.

The message of salvation in the Bible is not hard to understand (2 Cor. 4:3). Nevertheless we need to read it in a historical and global perspective so that we do not fall into indefensible private interpretations. Paul prays that his readers may "have power *together with all the saints* to grasp how wide and long and high and deep is the love of Christ and to know this love that surpasses knowledge" (Eph. 3:18).

### *The Bible and our relationship with God*

The Bible, as God's word, calls all people into relationship with God through repentance and forgiveness: listening to him, speaking to him, obeying him, and loving him. God does not only address us in direct speech: he also demonstrates what a relationship with him should be, as expressed in the experience of his people.

### *The Bible's authority and our response*

When a lukewarm Church opens the door (Rev. 3:20) and allows Jesus his full Lordship, the authority of the Bible will be felt immediately in daily life. Christians are transformed progressively into the likeness of Christ as they obey and are guided by Scripture. This entails both personal trust and holiness and also embarking on the mission to which God calls us: a mission of preaching good news and of reaching out with the costly love of Christ to make the world and human society pleasing to God.

As Christians *respond* to the authority of Scripture in these ways, they become more profoundly *aware* of its authority. Their obedience also *commends* the authority of Scripture to non-Christians:

showing that Scripture actually has authority, and that that authority belongs to a good God.

### The Bible's authority over the whole world

God's word is addressed to his world, not just to his Church. The Spirit caused it to be written in order to "convict the world of sin, of righteousness and of judgment." In accordance with this purpose, the Bible contains the only true message of salvation, which is in the name of Jesus Christ. The Bible warns the world about God's judgment of its sin, and proclaims the way of reconciliation.

## B. The Bible in Contemporary Cultures

All cultures have something God-given in them and have categories in which the gospel can begin to be understood. Yet every culture must be tested by Scripture and is under the judgment of God.

### The culture of modernity and post-modernity

Western society is characterized by modernity and post-modernity. Modernity is the culture of the enlightenment. It was confidently built on a foundation of the natural goodness of human beings, an evolutionary view of history and human progress, the myth of science and the construction of anthropocentric global utopias. These four provided a critique of all other world-views; but they proved unable to deliver the human progress they promised. Post-modernity does not disprove them so much as set other truths and authorities alongside them in an ideology of pluralism. But the culture of modernity is perpetuated in its institutions, including industrialization and education.

In this context, there are two poles to Western society. The first pole is that Western society has debunked and despises all authority. Traditional Western concepts of authority always required correcting by the Bible's concept of an authority based on love and suffering of the cross. Today, the very category 'authority' has been lost. The idea of the Bible's authority has become unintelligible.

The second pole is that at the same time, Western culture

pushes religion to the margins of public life. Unguided, people wander into privatized religion which is sometimes monist (confusing the divine and the human), sometimes seeks spiritual experience through physical ecstasy produced by drugs or sexual licence, and sometimes pursues false spiritualities such as occultism and New Age. Fulfilment is itself the goal of life, whether by moral or immoral ways.

In this culture the Church finds itself under real pressure. For the Church, the Bible is an authority that talks about morality; but the culture accepts neither authority nor morality.

In some areas the Church's own understanding, spirituality and practice has been affected by the culture of modernity. Some churches have permitted or encouraged marital infidelity and homosexual practice as means of 'living authentically' and so experiencing God. Such confusions have been common in human history. Hindu cultures knew of this in Tantric philosophy.

Western Christians need not let the culture of modernity paralyze their use of the Bible. They may affirm the authority of the Bible and let the Bible bring the culture of modernity and post-modernity under its own spotlight which shows that the same confusion of sex and religion was found in Baal religion. Although Western culture prides itself on its own modernity, the Bible's assessment of such a culture is that far from being in advance of other cultures, it is actually a regression. We cannot regard Western culture as being in the vanguard of progress.

### Syncretism

Societies which give their allegiance to a false god (religion or ideology) are under God's judgment. This false religion may be in the form of an organized cult or an unbiblical ideology such as modernity. In some cases these infect the Church with syncretism. This then questions the authority of Scripture in the Church as it creates a divided loyalty. It is necessary for God's people to choose whom they will serve (Exod. 20:3; Jo. 24:15).

### Is the Church powerless in the face of the culture of modernity?

Will the culture of modernity inevitably spread to and embrace other cultures? What is spreading is Western technology and institutions, powered by the institutions of capitalism, industrialism, the market, the media and educational institutions. Almost all nations are committed to embracing them.

However, non-Western cultures are responding to modernity in different ways. Some elements of the Islamic world resist it by reverting to fundamentalism, the force of which needs to be more fully appreciated. Hindu cultures absorb it like so many other challenges before. They absorb whatever they need and keep religion and family values firmly intact. Such cultures are confident of their ability to absorb what they wish from modernity and its benefits (some of which are undoubted) and to keep their soul and values intact. Thus it is not inevitable that Western difficulties with the concept of authority will be faced by all other cultures.

If even non-Christian cultures expect to survive the challenge of this culture, how much more should the authority of Scripture expect to prevail! The Church must challenge the modern world to enter the world of the Bible, and must place the culture of modernism in the spotlight of the Bible, so that its deficiencies can be exposed and it can be rejected or modified as this authority dictates.

## C. The Use of the Bible

The pressure of modernity does not mean we are to be paralyzed, unable to use the Bible and witness to its authority. Christians from Asia, Africa and Latin America in the consultation witnessed to the way they used the Bible. They found it effective in bringing people to acknowledge Christ as Lord and to join his people, in creating and affirming the humanity and dignity of people, and in strengthening morality and empowering effective mission. They have brought their worlds into the world of the Bible. The Bible itself affirms that there is nothing new under the sun. The world of post-modernity is a recent and powerful refinement of those fundamental lies on which rebellion against God are built. They challenge the Western Church to recover its confidence in the authority of the Bible.

One task of the people of God internationally, together as one community, is to be the 'Light of the world', shining the light of the biblical world-view onto the present world, including the culture of post-modernity. People thus discover who they really are in the light of the Bible. We do not have to make the Bible conform to the contexts we enter; we illuminate the contexts with the light of the Bible.

The authority of the Bible is both intrinsic and dynamic, finding its expression in biblical mission. Inter alia, this authority

- authorizes the Church to engage in mission
- enables us to describe the world as God sees it
- exposes the sinfulness of specific human contexts
- provides guidance, patterns, priorities and correction for mission in particular contexts
- is seen in its power to change people's lives as it is validated in transformed lives and the ethical distinctiveness of Christian individuals and communities.
- empowers Christians individually and corporately to witness to this life-changing power even in hostile contexts.
- must be the focus of theological education.

We have discussed the authority of Scripture with relation to practical Christian living — such as mission, evangelism, social concern, behaviour, and pastoral care. It has not been discussed in a vacuum or as an abstraction.

It is also understood in relation to specific cultures; and in particular to the concepts of authority and dominating values of those cultures. In some cultures 'authority' is heard as a liberating authorization of Christian proclamation and activity, in others it speaks of control and even oppression.

The Bible is God speaking to his people and his world. The world needs to listen and respond to the claims of the lordship of Christ or face the continuing onslaught of attacks on values which sustain humanity. The Bible gives humanity only two choices — to worship God or idols. All human life that is not focused on the worship of God and obedience to his word is, according to the Bible, in the thrall of idolatry, vulnerable to demonic influence in its structures and relationships, and finally self-destructive. To replace the image of God in humanity with a graven image demeans people. This is seen in various ways: in some cultures.

- sex is identified with religions;
- greed is exalted over compassion;
- children are brutalized in subtle ways;
- the reality of life is shunned in drugs or hedonism;
- materialistic cultures become models to be uncritically emulated;
- there is fear of evil spirits,
- political and economic oppression persists

To all humanity Scripture points the way because it points to Jesus Christ as Saviour and Lord. The fundamental authority is the Lordship of Jesus Christ, exalted to the right hand of God, through whom God now calls all people in all cultures to turn from their own way to the way, the truth and the life.

## D. The Impact of Scripture on Community and Personal Life

God's people express their submission to the authority of Scripture by the way their behaviour is transformed and shaped by God's will disclosed in Scripture. They must repent of the fact that evils in surrounding society are sometimes replicated in the Church. Particular current issues of behaviour include marital infidelity, homosexual practice, and corruption and graft which are present in all cultures, but especially visible in some. Complicity in the structural evils of surrounding society such as poverty, injustice, demeaning international structures of trade and degradation of the environment also contaminates the Church. Sin in these and other areas brings the name of Christ into disrepute.

The fundamental issue is however not immorality in the Church. The issue is the obedience or disobedience of the Church to the authority of Scripture, and to Jesus the Lord of Scripture and Church. Both the pressures of modernity and syncretism dilute the authority of Scripture and reinforce our unwillingness to obey it. The real issue is not the specific immoralities the Church exhibits, but its sinful disobedience to Scripture.

In Scripture itself, the will of God is to be modelled in the life of his people. This provides a vital witness to authority and its meaning. The practical impact of Scripture witnesses to its authority and will be seen in

- Personal holiness of life, including the quality of family life, marriage and gender relationships:
- Confident proclamation of the message of salvation;
- The mutual love of Christians and their unity in Christ;
- Critique of social, political and economic value systems, and competing understandings of truth;
- Care for the widow, the orphan, the stranger, the weak, the poor, and the chronically sick (especially those suffering from AIDS and its effects on families);
- The experience of suffering witnesses to the authority of our message when we are prepared to suffer for it;
- Witness to Government and society. We particularly noticed that the way the Two-Thirds World is using the Bible in the life of the nation is to take seriously the words of 1 Timothy 2:1-2, that prayers be made for those in authority to ensure peaceful and quiet lives in godliness and holiness. The Anglican churches have responded by taking a responsibility for the community in which are sent and for the nation they serve.

There was evidence from African and Asian churches of Governments turning to bishops for advice and also of other churches expecting the Anglican bishops to take a lead in affairs relating to Government and society.

Within the life of their nations, Christians have the opportunity to act as salt and light by responsible citizenship and by influencing national leaders. This opportunity has to be taken seriously, not only by the bishops but by the clergy and laity of our churches.

A concern for justice in society will be expressed in resistance to endemic corruption and bribery, to the production and export of goods that are injurious to health and the environment which are banned in the producing country, to the exploitation of labour and of women and children sexually, and to some of the policies of international corporations.

### Interpretation and the Practical Orientation of the Bible

For some the issue is not authority but interpretation. In the context of theological pluralism, we need a historical and global perspective on interpretation to save us from private interpretations.

The essential practicality of Scripture affects our attitude to the study of Scripture. We read it with all the available tools of scholarship to clarify its meaning; but are alert to prevent the authority of Scripture getting lost in the kind of study which never results in decisions which affect personal or social life. It is possible still to have the Bible but to have lost the Scripture.

### E. Scripture and Ecumenical Dialogue

Scripture can be used in ecumenical dialogue with full confidence in the consensus which Anglicans shared from Hooker to the Anglican Newman, namely:

- The Scriptures are sufficient for salvation;
- In this respect, they are utterly reliable;
- In the matter of saving truth, they are entirely perspicuous, even to the simple;
- The Scriptures are not prescriptive for every area of individual or church life; there is liberty to order personal, corporate and church life in the light of Scriptural principles;
- Authoritative teachers such as bishops can interpret Scripture and Tradition, yet are not infallible. Their teaching is to be received when it is manifestly consonant with Scripture and the apostolic tradition.

This position has won increasing respect from ecumenical dialogue partners, including both the Orthodox and post-Vatican II Catholicism. Evangelical Anglicans, especially EFAC, have a contribution to make in encouraging all Anglicans to remain faithful to this consensus, which now appears to offer the prospect of progress in ecumenical relations.

In this dialogue, faithfulness to the authority of Scripture and responsiveness to the pressing needs of mission and pastoral care, especially in parts of Africa, Asia and Latin America, presses on us yet again the urgency of a theological evaluation of the merits of delegated presidency of the eucharist.

At the same time, the lack within the WCC of a coherent theological rationale increases the yearning for a clear biblical basis. We encourage evangelicals to play the fullest part in WCC deliberations in order to meet this need.

## F. An International Network for Cross Cultural Mission

The Bible challenges the Church to be a missionary Church. Yet the Church in many parts of the world has yet to become involved in, and in other parts needs to be re-enthused about, international mission.

Consequently the Consultation Mission Track resolved to set up an *Evangelical Mission Resources International Network*. This is to encourage and facilitate evangelical Anglican involvement in world mission, including churches that are not yet so involved, and the cross-cultural movement of missionary personnel, through a networking of information and resources.

Bishops and mission leaders of churches in the South would like to develop the involvement of their dioceses, boards of mission or agencies in world mission, and hope progressively to take full responsibility for this involvement. They also see new needs for mission for which partners in the South are required. For this purpose they have proposed setting up a Network to be focussed on the cross-cultural location of long-term mission partners.

## G. Conclusion

We give thanks to God for the opportunity of consulting together, and for what we have learnt from his Word as we have read it together and sought to learn from our different perspectives. We offer this summary of our findings to our sisters and brothers throughout the Anglican Communion and beyond as we seek to obey Jesus Christ as Lord.

# Biblical Expositions
# The Anglican Communion
# and Scripture

*John Stott*

## 1. The God of Revelation (Isaiah 55)

I am thankful that the topic assigned for these biblical expositions is 'The Anglican Communion and Scripture'. For classical Anglicanism (at least as reformed and redefined in the sixteenth century) constantly affirms both the supremacy and the sufficiency of Scripture. That is to say, it is supreme in its authority over both the traditions of the church and the opinions of individuals, and it contains everything necessary for salvation, without any addition from outside.

Our first theme is 'The God of Revelation', and our text Isaiah 55.

Christianity is essentially a revealed religion. We affirm with joyful confidence and without embarrassment that we would know nothing about God if he had not made himself known. Indeed, if God had not revealed himself, we would not be Christians at all but rather Athenians, and all the world's altars would be inscribed 'to an unknown god'.

But we declare (as part of our distinctive evangelical witness, which we hold in trust for the rest of the church) that God has revealed himself – partly in the ordered loveliness of the created universe, supremely in Jesus Christ his incarnate Son, and also in the total biblical witness to Christ.

Isaiah 55 relates to the period when Israel was anticipating rescue from Babylonian exile. It divides itself naturally into three parts:

1. a three-fold portrait of the God of grace (vv.1-7)

2. this God is known only by revelation (vv.8-11)

3. the blessings enjoyed by those who believe in God's revelation (vv. 12 and 13)

Or, first the gracious character of God, secondly the spoken revelation of God, and thirdly the favoured people of God.

**The Gracious Character of God (vv. 1-7)**

Three amazing divine invitations are issued.

### *The thirsty are offered a free drink (vv. 1, 2)*

A messenger summons the people to a banquet. 'Come', he shouts in the streets, 'Come, if you are thirsty, to the waters. Come buy water, wine or milk, even if (paradoxically) you have no money to buy it with. Come, buy without money or cost. Why spend money on what does not satisfy, when you can get what does satisfy without money, for nothing?'

Here is the gracious gospel invitation, echoed by Jesus when he claimed to be the Bread of Life, and when he promised that those who came to him would never hunger or thirst; echoed by him again in the Beatitude which pronounces a blessing on those who are spiritually bankrupt; echoed again in the Parable of the Wedding Feast; and echoed finally in the last verses of the Book of Revelation: 'The Spirit and the bride say, "Come!" And let him who hears say, "Come!". Whoever is thirsty, let him come; and whoever wishes, let him take the free gift of the water of life.' (Rev. 22:17).

### *The nations are offered a free place in the covenant (vv. 3-7)*

God's covenant with David is recorded in 2 Samuel 7. It could not unjustly be described as nationalistic. For it promised that David's descendants would succeed him on the throne, and that his kingdom would be established for ever.

But now (v.4) the Messianic covenant is to be extended to the nations. For the Davidic Messiah will have a worldwide mission. He will summon the nations, and the nations will hasten to respond (v.5).

### The wicked are offered a free pardon (vv. 6, 7)

A wicked individual is addressed in verses 6 and 7, and urged in the following terms: 'Seek the Lord while he may be found; call on him while he is near. Let the wicked forsake his way and the evil man his thoughts. Let him turn to the Lord, and he will have mercy on him, and to our God, for he will freely pardon.'

Here then is displayed the gracious character of God. He offers a free drink to the thirsty, a free place to the nations, and a free pardon to the wicked. The emphasis is that each is free, the free drink, the free place, and the free pardon.

Who could have invented such a gospel? It is almost incredible, too good to be true! No human reasoning could have deduced it. No human speculation could have guessed it. For unenlightened human beings take it for granted that God has to be bribed into being favourable, and that salvation is by an accumulation of merit.

Only revelation could have disclosed the gracious character of God, and the free offer of his grace. As Micah put it, when the nations come crawling in fear to Yahweh: 'Who is a God like you, who pardons sin and forgives the transgression of the remnant of his inheritance? You do not stay angry for ever but delight to show mercy.' (Micah 7:18).

So this (the necessity of revelation) is what the prophet comes to next.

## The Spoken Revelation of God (vv. 8-11)

As the prophet reflects on the grace of God to the thirsty, the nations and the wicked, he realises that he could know it only by revelation. He hears Yahweh saying so in four affirmations:

### Yahweh's thoughts and ways are inaccessible to us

'For my thoughts are not your thoughts, neither are your ways my ways', declares the Lord (v.8). Indeed, 'as the heavens are higher than the earth, so are my ways higher than your ways and my thoughts than your thoughts' (v.9). The thoughts in the mind of God are as much higher than the thoughts in our minds as the heavens are higher than the earth. And that means infinity. The gulf between God's mind and ours is unbridgeable. Of course our minds (our rationality being part of the divine image in us) are capable of remarkable achievements in the realm of the empirical sciences. But when we are seeking God and the way of salvation, our minds flounder helplessly out of their depth. How could we ever find God or discover the way of salvation by ourselves? Our little minds cannot climb up into the infinite mind of God. There is no ladder by which we can reach him. We need to humble ourselves at his feet, to confess our ignorance, and to acknowledge our need of revelation.

### *Yahweh's lofty thoughts must come down to us*

They must come down to our level, if we are ever to grasp them. V.10 begins with a reference to the rain and the snow, which 'come down from heaven' and water the earth. Notice this second reference to both heaven and earth. According to v.9 God's thoughts are as much higher than ours as the heaven is higher than the earth. According to v.10 as the rain and the snow bring blessing down from heaven to earth, so Yahweh's thoughts come down to us. In other words, if we are ever to know his thoughts (which tower high above ours), he must take the initiative and bring them down to us.

### *Yahweh's thoughts have come down to us;*
### *they have been put into words*

The prophet moves from the thoughts in the mind of God (vv.8-10) to the words spoken by the mouth of God (v.11). Thus Scripture itself uses human speech as its model of revelation. Speech is the most direct and flexible medium of human communication. It is by the words of our mouth that we communicate the thoughts of our minds. Why, we cannot even read each other's minds unless we speak. If I were to stand here silent, see if you can read my thoughts. It is impossible!

But now, at this moment, you do know exactly what is going on in my mind, because I am speaking to you. I am conveying to you the thoughts of my mind by means of the words of my mouth.

It is an excellent illustration of the necessity of divine revelation. If we cannot read each other's minds unless we speak, how much less could we read God's infinite mind unless he speaks! But God has spoken! His word has gone forth from his mouth. He has clothed his thoughts in words. Like snow and rain coming down to the earth, so God's words have brought his thoughts down to us.

*Yahweh's word is powerful; it always achieves its purpose*

We look at v.10 again: 'As the rain and the snow come down from heaven, and do not return to it without watering the earth and making it bud and flourish, so that it yields seed for the sower and bread for the eater, so (v.11) is my word that goes out from my mouth: it will not return to me empty, but will accomplish what I desire and achieve the purpose for which I sent it.'

Thus God's word is living and active, and sharper than any two-edged sword (Hebrews 4:12). Again, 'the word of God ... is at work in you who believe' (1 Thess. 2:13).

It is by the word of God that the universe came into being and is sustained in being, and it is equally by the word of God that he saves those who believe, yes and sanctifies them too, and brings them to glory.

To sum up the teaching of vv.8-11 in four stages: God's thoughts, which are inaccessible to us, have been brought down to us, within our reach. For God has spoken them, and his word is powerfully effective in fulfilling his purpose.

## The Favoured People of God (vv. 12, 13)

Happy indeed are the people to whom God has spoken! Vv. 12 and 13 describe in vivid Hebrew poetic imagery the immense blessings enjoyed by the people of God who have received and now believe the word of God.

First, they will experience a new Exodus (v.12). They will 'go out' (now from Babylon as they had done from Egypt) 'with both joy and peace. The mountains and hills will burst into song ... , and all the trees of the field will clap their hands.'

Secondly, they will inherit a new Promised Land (v.13). In place of useless thorns and briars (symbols of the curse of Genesis

3, following the Fall), lovely pine trees and myrtle trees will grow, and the salvation of God's people will be for Yahweh's eternal renown.

## Conclusion

We have a tragic tendency to allow the gospel to become prosaic and ordinary, as tawdry as a junk shop, as flat as uncorked champagne. It is urgent that we recover its freshness, its lustre, its sparkle, its fizz.

The truth of the gospel is so amazing as to be all but incredible. It tells us that God reaches out to us in free grace, to the thirsty, the nations and the wicked, to those who deserve nothing at his hand but judgment, to those who have no merit to plead and no contribution to make.

We could never have known, or even guessed, this good news apart from revelation. But God has revealed it, and it is true! So the message we have to share in the world mission of the church is not our own threadbare speculations; it is the revelation of God. It is not some tame little twopenny twaddle; it is God's good news for the world.

# 2. Light in the Darkness (2 Peter 1:12 -21)

In this text Peter makes four important affirmations about Scripture. True, the first two are about the apostles (himself and his fellow apostles), affirming that they were eye-witnesses of Christ (vv. 12-18), while the second two are about the prophets of the Old Testament (vv. 19-21). In fact, with the benefit of hindsight, we may say that vv. 12-18, containing the witness of the apostles, are about the New Testament, while vv. 19-21, containing the witness of the prophets, are about the Old Testament. Nevertheless, what Peter writes about either group is also true of the other. So the whole paragraph is about the Bible, since the Bible unites the prophets and the apostles, Old Testament and New Testament, in a single book, which is their common witness to Christ.

## Biblical Truth is Written Truth (vv. 12-15)

It is of course obvious that biblical truth is written truth, since the word 'Scripture' means precisely 'what is written'. In order to understand the point which Peter is making, we need to notice the combination of the human background and the divine providence.

### *The human background is the mortality of the apostle Peter*

Peter is anticipating his approaching death. In v.13 he describes himself as 'living in the tent of this body'. In v.14 he adds that he knows he will soon put it aside, as our Lord Jesus Christ had made clear to him (a reference probably to John 21:18ff). In v.15 he refers to his 'departure', meaning his death.

So the apostle is vividly conscious of the transience of his earthly life. He refers to his life as 'camping', living in a tent, and to his death as folding up his tent and moving on.

Why was he so concerned about this? His mortality was not a personal problem to him; his anxiety was for his readers. Let me explain. Peter was an apostle of Jesus Christ, chosen and sent by him to teach in his name. Now that he was approaching death, however, what would happen to his teaching then? That was the question.

While Peter was still alive, he could and would remind the people of his teaching. Twice he says so. V.12: 'I will always remind you of these things, even though you know them and are firmly established in the truth you now have'. V.13: 'I think it is right to refresh your memory as long as I live in the tent of this body'.

But because he would soon die, he would make every effort to ensure that after his departure his teaching would still be available to them; and they would always be able to remember it. V.15 contains a third reference to their memory.

So this was the responsible policy of an apostle, who knew that Christ had called him to a unique teaching role. While he was alive, he would continue to teach and to remind them, but after his death they would have his teaching in writing.

What was he referring to? Probably not to his two letters, because they had already been written, and it is a future writing

ministry to which he is referring. So perhaps it is a reference to
the Gospel of Mark, which may not yet have been published. The
early church father Papias said that Mark was Peter's translator
or interpreter. Irenaeus described Mark as 'a disciple and interpreter of Peter', who handed down in writing the substance of
Peter's preaching.

Anyway, this was the human background – Peter's conscious
mortality, and his decision to write down his teaching for the
benefit of posterity.

### The divine providence which lay behind it

If God had said something and done something through Jesus
Christ, which was decisive for the salvation of the world, then it
is inconceivable that he should allow this unique word and deed
to be lost in the mists of antiquity. No. If God said and did
something definitive and final in Christ, he must have made
provision for it to be preserved, so that future generations in
every place could have access to it.

This is why, in his loving providence, God caused what had
been spoken to be written. Indeed, this is the overriding purpose
of Scripture. Scripture is 'God's word written' (Article 21). It is
therefore available for the blessing of all people at all times in all
places.

## Biblical Truth is Eye-witness Truth (vv. 16-18)

V.16b: 'We told you about the power and coming of our Lord
Jesus Christ', his 'power' being perhaps a reference to his ministry on earth, and his 'coming' undoubtedly a reference to the
*parousia* of his glory. Moreover, in telling the people about these
things, 'we did not follow cleverly invented stories' or fairy tales,
since we did not make it up. On the contrary, 'we were eye-
witnesses of his majesty'.

This is a very important expression. We need to consider both
the principle behind it and the illustration of the Transfiguration
which Peter supplies.

### The principle, or the need for eye-witnesses

This is a principle which applies to the whole of Scripture. All
the biblical authors were to some degree eye-witnesses of God's

work. Take the Old Testament prophets. They were eye-witnesses of what God was doing in their day, both judging the
nations and saving and judging Israel. In fact, God deliberately
raised up the prophets in order to be his witnesses, to watch what
he was doing, to record it, and to interpret or explain it.

In the same way, Jesus chose and called the apostles, in order
that they might be 'with him' (Mark 3:14), in order to hear his
words, see his acts, and then bear witness to what they had seen
and heard.

The reason was this. God's mighty acts of salvation and
judgment, whether in the Old Testament or in the New, were not
explicit enough to stand by themselves; their meaning was not
self-evident. They needed interpretation.

For example, there were many tribal migrations in the Ancient Near East. Peoples were constantly on the move. So in that
sense the Exodus was not unique. Nobody would have known
that the Exodus of Israel from Egypt was in any way special,
leading to the covenant, unless God had raised up Moses to
record and explain it.

Again, hundreds of thousands of crucifixions took place in
Palestine under Roman rule. In that sense the cross of Jesus was
not unique. So nobody would ever have known that the crucifixion of Jesus of Nazareth was special, indeed the pivot of the
world's salvation, unless the apostles had been raised up to
record and explain it.

So much for the principle, namely the need for eye-witnesses
to see, record and explain what God was doing.

### *The example: the Transfiguration*

The Transfiguration of Jesus was specially important because
it gave the apostles a preview both of his resurrection body and
of his *parousia* glory. Peter was one of the privileged three who
were there. 'We were eye-witnesses of his majesty', he wrote.
They not only saw the glory; they also heard the voice, God the
Father giving him honour and glory and acknowledging him as
his Son (v.17). V.18: 'We ourselves heard this voice ... when we
were with him on the sacred mountain'.

We thank God, therefore, that the Bible is the testimony of

specially appointed eye-witnesses, who heard and saw what God was doing, and then from their experience recorded and explained it. We thank God also that the Gospels contain the words and works of Jesus and that the Gospel writers were either themselves eye-witnesses or (specially in the case of Luke) obtained their information from eye-witnesses. The reliability of Scripture, from a human point of view, is due to the integrity of the biblical eye-witnesses.

## Biblical Truth is Enlightening Truth

V.19a: 'and we have the word of the prophets made more certain'. Perhaps this is a reference to the Gospels, which confirm the reliability of the Old Testament prophets by recording how their prophecies were fulfilled. V.19b: 'and you will do well to pay attention to it, as to a light shining in a dark place, until the day dawns and the morning star rises in your hearts'.

This is a marvellous metaphor. God's word is likened to a bright light in a dark place. The people of God are pictured as pilgrims, travelling by night. On that account we are liable to stumble, and even to go astray. We need a lamp to illumine our path. And God has given one to us. Already in Psalm 119:105 his word is called 'a lamp to my feet and a light for my path'. Now Peter emphasizes that the darkness of the world around us makes this lamp even more necessary.

To be sure, we shall not need it for ever, because the darkness will not last for ever. One day the dawn will break, and the morning star will rise over the horizon. In other words, Jesus Christ will come, and the fullness of his light will shine upon us, for we shall see him face to face. But meanwhile, until that day dawns, we would be wise to pay attention to the light which God has given us.

I think we can learn two lessons from the fact that Scripture is likened to a lamp.

### *Scripture has a practical purpose*

A torch or flashlight has a practical purpose. It tells us not only where we are, but where we should be going, and how to avoid pitfalls on the way.

Just so Scripture tells us what to believe and how to behave.

It illumines our path; it directs our way. It shows us how to walk through this dark world. Thank God we have a lamp! It does not always give us detailed instructions about complex contemporary issues. But it lays down principles which are often illustrated, and which can be applied to our modern dilemmas.

## Scripture is a simple book

True, it contains difficult passages and doctrines. Peter goes on to write in chapter 3, v.16, that he himself finds some things in Paul's letters 'hard to understand'. But these are the exceptions. Generally speaking, and especially regarding the central message of the Bible, namely the way of salvation, Scripture is plain. Indeed, it is 'perspicuous'; that is, it has a see-through, transparent quality. For God spoke in order to communicate, and not in order to confuse. So we must not turn Scripture into a book of puzzles and enigmas. No, we look for the plain, natural, obvious meaning of the text. We pay attention to it as to a light shining in the darkness.

## Biblical Truth is Divine Truth (vv. 20, 21)

These verses are a beautiful example of the balance of the Bible, especially in the matter of the relation between God and man, the divine and the human, in the production of Scripture.

### A double assertion about Scripture

This is found in the negative and positive clauses of vv. 20 and 21, which complement one another and which insist that the origin of Scripture was in God not in human beings.

Negatively, 'above all, ... no prophecy of Scripture came about by the prophet's own interpretation'. Also v.21a: 'for prophecy never had its origin in the will of man ... '. This double negative statement is fundamental. We reject any notion that the Bible is a purely human book, which belongs alongside other books and is due to the literary genius of human beings. No, no. However we should translate v.20 (and this is not certain), it will be a safe principle to take the two negative clauses together. That is, no prophecy originated in either the mind or the will of the prophet. The initiative in speaking or writing was never their own. They neither thought it up in their own mind, nor decided what to speak by their own will. They never said: 'Well, it is a fine day today, so I think I will do a little prophesying'!

Instead, and positively (v.21b), 'men (possibly 'holy men') spoke from God (by his initiative, his command and his authority) as they were carried along by the Holy Spirit.'

B B Warfield wrote of this verse in his justly famous essay 'The Biblical Idea of Inspiration'. He drew attention to other New Testament uses of the participle *pheromenos*, translated here 'carried along'. In Acts 2:2 this is the word for the 'rushing' or 'blowing' of the mighty wind on the Day of Pentecost. In Acts 27, when the ship was caught in the Mediterranean storm, and could not head into the wind, the crew gave into it. In consequence, 'we were driven along' (*epherometha*, v.15), and 'they ... let the ship be driven along' (*epheronto*, v.17). In other words, the ship drifted at the mercy of the wind.

The implication of this is clear. As the ship was driven by the wind to a destination determined by the wind, not the ship, so the prophets were carried along by the Holy Spirit and inspired to say things determined by him, not by them. As B B Warfield put it, they were 'taken up by the Holy Spirit and brought by his power to the goal of his choosing' (p.137).

It is impossible to miss what is being affirmed here. The double statement about Scripture is that it originated not in human minds and wills, but in the mind and will of God.

However, as we consider carefully what Peter is writing, we need to add an important qualification or explanation, arising from his statement that 'men spoke from God'.

### *The double authorship of Scripture, or its 'co-authorship' (B B Warfield, p. 173)*

Although no Scripture originated in the mind or will of human beings, that does not mean that it altogether by-passed their minds and wills. Although they were carried along by the Holy Spirit, they were not so overpowered by the Spirit as to be deprived of thought and speech. No. Although 'men spoke from God', yet they did speak.

In fact, 2 Peter 1:21 invites comparison with Hebrews 1:1. According to Hebrews 1:1 '*God* spoke through the prophets', whereas according to 2 Peter 1:21 *'prophets* spoke from God'. Of course these are two ways of saying the same thing. Yet the emphasis is not the same. For the subject of the verb to 'speak' is different. In Hebrews 1 *God* spoke, whereas in 2 Peter 1 *men* spoke.

So then, is the Bible the word of God because he spoke it? Or is it the word of men because they spoke it? The biblical answer is both, namely that God spoke through men, or men spoke from God. The Bible is both the word of God and the word of men. Better, it is the word of God through the words of men. It is of great importance to preserve the double authorship of Scripture, since this is the Bible's own account of itself, and not to affirm either in such a way as to deny the other.

So the process of inspiration (however mysterious, for Scripture nowhere describes its mechanics) involved the concurrent operation of the divine Spirit and the human authors. The Holy Spirit treated them as persons, not machines. He respected their personality and did not violate it. Consequently, they engaged in historical researches, had their own literary styles, and made their own theological emphases, which were appropriate to their own personality and experience. At the same time, even while they were researching and reflecting, and writing in a manner that was appropriate to them, the Holy Spirit was carrying them forward to express what was intended by him. We must never affirm either truth in such a way as to deny the other.

Thus, on the one hand God spoke, deciding himself what he wanted to say, yet not in such a way as to distort the personality of the human authors. On the other hand, men spoke, using their human faculties freely, yet not in such a way as to distort the message of the divine author. As Dr J I Packer has written, this is 'the biblical idea of God's *concursive operation* in, with and through the free working of man's own mind' (*Fundamentalism and the Word of God*, 1958, p. 82).

### A double approach to Scripture

The double authorship of Scripture demands a double approach. It determines how we understand the command to 'pay attention' to it (v.19).

Because Scripture is the word of God, we read it like no other book, humbly, on our knees, crying to the Holy Spirit for illumination. Because Scripture is also the word of men, we read it like every other book, paying attention to its historical and geographical background, its cultural context, its literary genre, its grammar, syntax and vocabulary. We study it diligently.

These two approaches, the humble and the diligent or thoughtful, are not incompatible with one another. In the Old Testament we read that Daniel 'set his mind to gain understanding and humbled himself before God' (Daniel 10:12). In the New Testament Paul told Timothy to 'reflect' on what he was saying, and then the Lord would give him 'insight' into everything (2 Timothy 2:7).

I recapitulate. Biblical truth is (1) written truth (Scripture is God's word written), (2) eye-witness truth (the authors bearing witness to what they had seen and heard), (3) enlightening truth (like a lamp shining in a dark place), and (4) divine truth (the word of God through the words of men).

Now let me restate these four truths in their chronological order, so that we may better grasp the providence of God.

First, certain things happened (God's mighty acts in the history of Israel, in the saving career of Jesus, and in the ministry of the apostles), which were witnessed and explained by God's appointed spokespersons. Secondly, they were written down for the benefit of subsequent generations throughout the world. Thirdly, this process of writing was a divine-human activity called 'inspiration', men speaking from God and God speaking through men. Fourthly, the resulting product, 'the prophetic word' or 'Scripture', shines like a light in a dark place, and is given to illumine the path of Christian pilgrims, until the glorious daybreak when Christ appears.

## Conclusion

Two responses will be appropriate in conclusion. First, let us praise God for his word! It is a most marvellous provision for our need.

Secondly, let us pay close attention to it! With what painstaking care we should study the very words of God! Has God condescended to speak, and shall we not listen? Has he caused what he has spoken to be written, and shall we not read it? Has he given us a light to shine in the darkness, and shall we not walk by it? 'You will do well to pay attention to it' (middle of v.19). It is a good thing to do so. And those who do will surely receive that most coveted of all accolades: 'Well done, good and faithful servant!'.

# 3. The Spirit of Truth (John 14-16)

Our topic is the work of the Holy Spirit and the production of Scripture, as Jesus threw light on it in the Upper Room discourse. The Upper Room discourse holds a special place of respect and affection in the hearts and minds of Christian people. For these were among the Saviour's last words. So understandably we cherish them.

It is well-known that within this discourse are included five paragraphs about the work of the Holy Spirit, two in John 14, one in John 15 and two more in John 16. Moreover, three times in these paragraphs Jesus gave the Holy Spirit the title 'the Spirit of truth' (14:16,17; 15:26; 16:13). And in each of the five paragraphs, even when He is not called 'the Spirit of truth', some allusion is made to His teaching or testifying ministry. Thus 'truth' is attributed to the Father ('the only true God'), the Son ('I am the truth') and the Holy Spirit ('the Spirit of truth').

The fact that Jesus called the Holy Spirit 'the Spirit of truth', and gave such a prominent place to his teaching ministry, is of great importance in the anti-intellectual cultures of the world. I do not hesitate to say that anti-intellectualism and the fullness of the Holy Spirit are mutually incompatible, because the Spirit with whom we claim to be filled or desire to be filled is the Spirit of truth. In consequence where the Holy Spirit is free to work, truth matters.

In these chapters Jesus describes six ministries of the Spirit of truth.

### 'The Spirit will teach you all things' (14:26)

At the risk of shocking you, I must immediately say that this is not so! 'But', you may protest, 'how dare you contradict the explicit words of Jesus?' Well, this text gives us the opportunity to affirm that evangelical people are not biblical literalists, and do not believe that every word of the Bible is literally true. For example, we cannot insist that 'all things' means all things in an absolute and unqualified sense.

If the Holy Spirit had taught us all things, then of course we would know all things. But we are not infallible, let alone omniscient. On the contrary, as Paul said, 'Now we see only the dim reflections of a mirror', and, as John said, 'We do not yet know what we shall be'.

So we bring discredit on our evangelical cause when we give the impression that we are cocky little know-alls. I would like to see more evangelical humility among us, and a greater readiness to say 'I don't know'. Deuteronomy 29:29 remains a verse of great importance. It divides truth into two categories, namely 'the revealed things' and 'the secret things'. In consequence, Christians ought to be healthy blend of dogmatism and agnosticism, dogmatic about what has been clearly revealed and agnostic about what has been kept secret. Indeed, our troubles begin when we allow our dogmatism to trespass into the realm of secret things or our agnosticism into the realm of the revealed things.

How then do we interpret Jesus' statement that the Holy Spirit would teach us 'all things'? He must have meant 'all things which it is the Father's will for us to know'. In other words, the statement is relative rather than absolute.

### 'The Spirit will remind you of everything I have said to you' (14:25, 26)

We need to note the repetition of a particular phrase in these verses, namely the three words 'I have spoken'. Jesus was understandably concerned about what he had spoken to his disciples. For three years he had been teaching them. He had left them a rich patrimony of truth. So now he promises that after he has gone the Father will send the Holy Spirit, not only to go on teaching them, but also to remind them of everything which he had taught them.

It is a text, I know, which Christians with bad memories have latched on to! And I suppose it could be given a secondary application to the task of Scripture memorisation. But the primary reference of this promise is different. Five times Jesus uses the pronoun 'you': 'all this I have spoken to *you* while still with *you*. But ... the Holy Spirit ... will teach *you* all things and will remind *you* of everything I have said to *you* '. It is clear then that the people whom the Holy Spirit will remind are the same people whom Jesus has taught, namely the apostles. Jesus had done the teaching; the Holy Spirit would do the reminding.

The most obvious fulfilment of this promise was in the writing of the Gospels. Evangelical scholars are rightly engaged in 'Gospel criticism' (which means not that they criticise the Gospels, but that they investigate their sources, forms, concerns etc.), and they need our encouragement to persevere in their studies.

At the same time, I hope that they neither they nor we will be shy of adding what liberal scholars normally omit, namely that alongside the human mechanics of gospel composition, the Holy Spirit himself was reminding the apostles of what Jesus had spoken to them. For Jesus himself was concerned that his teaching should be preserved for the benefit of future generations.

### "The Spirit will testify about me' (15:26)

Jesus has been talking about the opposition of the world. 'If the world hates you, keep in mind that it hated me first' (v.18). Again, 'no servant is greater than his master. If they persecuted me, they will persecute you also' (v.20). Moreover, this was in fulfilment of Psalm 69 verse 4 which says 'they hated me without reason' (v.25).

Only now does Jesus move on, almost abruptly to the coming and the ministry of the Holy Spirit. 'When the Counsellor comes ..., the Spirit of truth ..., he will testify about me' (v.26). So the testimony which Jesus has in mind will be given in an evangelistic context. It is before an unbelieving and hostile world that the Holy Spirit bears his testimony to Jesus.

This should help us in evangelism to get things in proportion. We sometimes make too much of our own 'testimony', by which we often mean 'autobiography'. And personal testimony is important, even necessary. But in order of priority we are the third witnesses. The first and chief witness to Jesus in the world is the Holy Spirit himself: 'he will testify about me'. The second witness is that of the apostles: and you also must testify, for you have been with me from the beginning (v.27). They had been chosen by Jesus in order to be with him, to hear his words, see his works and so bear witness to what they had seen and heard. Only then, after the witness of the Spirit and the testimony of the apostolic eye-witnesses, comes our own witness. It is in the third place. It confirms from our own experience the witness of the Spirit through the apostles in the New Testament.

### 'The Spirit will convict the world of sin, righteousness and judgment' (16:8-11)

Here is another ministry of the Spirit to the unbelieving world. He convicts the world (that is, convinces it by evidence and argument) concerning three truths. If I may over simplify, he convinces the world of the gravity of their sin and guilt, of the possibility of righteousness, and of the certainty of coming judgment. He makes these three moral categories, of which the world customarily makes light, a solemn reality to people. And in each case he produces evidence to secure conviction. He convinces the world of sin because they do not believe in Jesus; of righteousness, because he is going to the Father and his resurrection/ascension will vindicate his work on the cross; and of judgment, because the prince of this world has already been judged, decisively overthrown at the cross and the resurrection.

This paragraph is an important counterpart to the end of chapter 15. For the Spirit's conviction of sin and the Spirit's testimony to Christ belong inseparably together. It is only those whose eyes have been opened to see the reality of sin, righteousness and judgment, who are ready to see the corresponding reality of Christ as the Saviour from sin.

### 'The Spirit will guide you into all truth' (16:13)

It is mainly because of this statement in its implications that I have chosen John 14 to 16 for our reflections this morning, because today's conference topic is 'Scripture and Ecumenical

Dialogue'. And John 16 vv. 12 and 13 are significant verses in regard to the claims of the different churches and relations between the churches on the basis of their claims. I would go further. These verses constitute a key text in ecumenical encounter. Indeed, I doubt if any text has suffered from a greater variety of interpretations, and from more misinterpretation, even manipulation, than this one.

The question at issue concerns the identity of the 'you' in the promise 'the Spirit will guide you into all truth'. Whom does the Holy Spirit lead into all the truth? There are three or four major interpretations – Catholic, Liberal, Pentecostal and Evangelical.

First, the Catholic interpretation is that 'you' means the Catholic hierarchy, the Pope surrounded by his college of bishops as the successors of the apostles. They claim that Jesus gave them a magisterium based on this promise, and carrying with it a guarantee of infallibility.

Secondly, the Liberal interpretation is that 'you' means each individual Christian. Jesus promised, they claim, that the Holy Spirit would guide each individual through his or her reason, conscience and experience into the truth.

Thirdly, it is not unfair, I think, to add that some Pentecostal and Charismatic people (both individuals and groups) make a similar claim to a knowledge of the truth based on Jesus' promise of the Spirit. He has led them into all the truth, they claim, even into new truth which goes beyond the teaching of Scripture.

We need the courage and clarity to reject these three interpretations in favour of a fourth.

The Evangelical interpretation, which is based on the principle of history, insists that the 'you' refers to the apostles, gathered round Jesus in the Upper Room. His promise was fulfilled in the writing of the New Testament, in which the apostles display astonishing insight, which the Twelve never had during the Jesus' public ministry.

The argument is this: the pronoun 'you' occurs three times in one sentence, and the identity of this 'you' cannot change in the middle of a single sentence. Here is v.12: 'I have much more to say to you, more than you can now bear'. In other words, Jesus regarded his teaching ministry to the apostles as incomplete. He had much more that he wanted to teach them, but they were dull of hearing and could not take it. So he went on: 'But when he the Spirit of truth comes, he will guide you into all truth' (v.13). That is, the Holy Spirit would do what Jesus had been unable to do. He would complete what Jesus had left incomplete. He would lead them into all truth, not in absolute sense (as in 14 v.26), but into all truth which Jesus had wanted to teach them, but had been unable to.

This great promise was fulfilled in the writing of the New Testament, especially the Epistles and the Revelation. As we read these writings, especially Peter and John, with all their rich profundity of insight, when they had been so blind and dull before, we ask ourselves: where did they get all this from? Our answer is that it came from the Holy Spirit, who led them into all the truth.

We are now in a position to bring together John 14 vv.25, 26 and John 16 vv.12,13, together with the promises of Jesus which they contain. John 14 v.25 refers to what Jesus had said to them, and John 16 v.12 refers to what he had wanted to say to them, but had not been able to say. Similarly, John 14 v.26 is a promise that the Holy Spirit would remind them of everything he Jesus had taught them, while John 16 v.13 is a promise that the Holy Spirit would supplement what he had said, by leading them into all the truth, and so teaching them what he had not been able to teach. Thus John 14 alludes to the Holy Spirit's reminding ministry, and John 16 to the Holy Spirit's supplementing ministry. The promise of the reminding Spirit was fulfilled in the writing of the Gospels, and the promise of the supplementing Spirit was fulfilled in the writing of the Epistles.

This is not to say that the Holy Spirit has been idle since the post apostolic period began, but rather that his ministry has changed. He did lead the apostles into all the truth, which is now contained in the New Testament. Since then he has been leading the church into an understanding of that truth. His ministry to the apostles was one of revelation; his ministry to the post apostolic church was one of illumination, enlightening the church of each new generation to grasp more of what he had revealed

### 'The Spirit will glorify me' (16:14)

The promise that the Holy Spirit would 'glorify' Jesus, means that he would manifest him or make him known, for he would take from what belonged to Christ and make it known to them.

So the major concern of the Holy Spirit in the Scriptures has been to bear witness to Christ. 'It is they which bear witness to me', he said (Jn. 5:39).

And the Holy Spirit's ministry remains a fundamentally Christ-centred ministry. His two major concerns are to show Christ to us and to form Christ in us.

It is safe to say that the Holy Spirit is a shy, retiring and reticent Spirit. Tom Smail has called him 'the self-effacingness of God'. He dislikes publicity. His overriding desire is to glorify Christ. As A W Tozer wrote, the Holy Spirit 'is drawn to the sweet Name of Jesus as bees are drawn to the fragrance of clover.' Or as Dr J I Packer has written 'the Holy Spirit's distinctive new covenant role ... is to fulfil what we may call a floodlight ministry in relation to the Lord Jesus Christ ... When floodlighting is well done, the floodlights are so placed that you do not see them ...; what you are meant to see is just the building on which the floodlights are trained ...' So the Spirit is 'the hidden floodlight shining on the Saviour'.

It seems to me that this truth could be a great help in building more mutually accepting and respectful relationships between charismatic and non-charismatic evangelicals. If we could agree (1) that the Holy Spirit does not appreciate being lionized or publicized; (2) that he delights rather in bringing honour and glory to Jesus, and (3) that we should talk more of Christ and less of the Spirit, – then – we should be able to find in Christ the unity which often eludes us when we focus on the Spirit.

We have seen that Jesus spoke in the Upper Room discourse of the ministry of the Holy Spirit as 'the Spirit of truth'. We have also seen that this ministry consists of teaching ('he will teach ...'), reminding ('he will bring to your remembrance ...'), witnessing ('he will bear witness to me ...'), convicting ('he will convince the world'), revealing ('he will lead you into all truth') and glorifying ('he will glorify me').

It is a beautifully comprehensive, multi-faceted ministry. And although in the Upper Room discourse Jesus is focussing on his unique ministry to the apostles, yet in secondary ways he can be 'the Spirit of truth' to us as well.

### Conclusion

In conclusion, I think we may learn four simple truths. Firstly, truth matters. The Holy Spirit is the Spirit of truth, who desires to lead people into the truth. We must never denigrate the importance of truth.

Secondly, the Holy Spirit had a unique ministry to the apostles, both reminding them of the teaching of Jesus and supplementing it. It is thus that he constituted the New Testament.

Thirdly, the heart of the New Testament is Christ. The Holy Spirit both witnesses to Christ before the world and glorifies Christ in the church.

Fourthly, the same Holy Spirit, who revealed Christ objectively to the apostles, now illumines our minds to understand ever more of his revelation.

# 4. The Holy Spirit and the Holy Bible (1 Corinthians 2:6-16)

All Christians know that the Holy Bible and the Holy Spirit are supposed to have something to do with one another. Indeed, we believe that the Holy Bible is the creative product of the Holy Spirit. As the Nicene Creed puts it, 'he spoke through the prophets. It is the relationship between the Spirit and the Bible which we are to investigate, and in particular the part played by the Holy Spirit in the composition of Scripture. For Christians have a Trinitarian understanding of Scripture. It comes from God; it focusses on Christ; it is inspired by the Holy Spirit. The Bible is the Father's witness to the Son through the Spirit.

Our text is 1 Corinthians 2:6-16, and we must set the text in its context. Up to this point in 1 Corinthians Paul has been emphasizing the 'foolishness' of the gospel (e.g. 1:18, 23).

So now Paul adds a kind of corrective, lest the Corinthians should think that he repudiates wisdom altogether, and glories in folly instead. Was the apostle Paul an anti-intellectual after all? Did he scorn understanding and the place of the mind? No. We look at verses 6 and 7:

'We do however speak a message of wisdom among the mature, but not the wisdom of this age ... No, we speak of God's secret wisdom, a wisdom that has been hidden and that God destined for our glory before time began.'

In other words, we do impart wisdom, he says, but with three important qualifications.

First, it is wisdom for the mature (*teleioi*), not for the unregenerate, nor even for babes in Christ, since it is solid food which they cannot digest (3:1, 4).

Secondly, it is God's wisdom not the wisdom of this age, or the wisdom of the world.

Thirdly, it is wisdom designed or destined for our glory. That is, it is not just good news of justification; it concerns our glorification, our final perfection through sharing the glory of God.

All this means that in evangelism we proclaim the foolishness of the cross. We resolve to know nothing but Christ and him crucified, and through the folly of the *kerygma* God saves those who believe. In Christian nurture, however, building people up into maturity, we want them to understand God's total purpose, what in v.7 Paul calls 'God's secret wisdom' and in v.9 'what God has prepared for those who love him'.

This wisdom can be known only by revelation. 'The rulers of this age' (secular leaders) did not understand it, or they would never have crucified the Lord of glory (v.8). They were not exceptional, however. All human beings, if left to themselves, are ignorant of God's wisdom and purpose. Paul insists on this in v.9, which is a quotation from Isaiah 64:4. God's wisdom, he says, is something which no eye has seen (it is invisible), no ear has heard (it is inaudible) and no mind has imagined (it is inconceivable). It is altogether beyond the reach of our eyes, ears and minds. It is amenable neither to scientific investigation, nor to poetic imagination. It is absolutely unattainable by our little, fallen, finite, fallible minds – unless God should reveal himself, which is exactly what he has done!

Listen to vv.9 and 10 again: 'No eye has seen, no ear has heard, no mind has conceived what God has prepared for those who love him – but God has revealed it to us by his Spirit'. The word 'us' is emphatic, and in the context must refer not to all of us indiscriminately, but to the apostle Paul who is writing, and by extension to his fellow apostles. God had given a special revelation to them. One is reminded of Ephesians 3:5, where 'the mystery of Christ' (namely, the incorporation of Jews and Gentiles into the body of Christ on the same terms) 'has now been revealed by the Spirit to God's holy apostles and prophets'.

This, then, is the context. It is a rather lengthy introduction to what follows, in which Paul gives a comprehensive statement of the Holy Spirit's work as agent of divine revelation. The Holy Spirit is presented to us in four stages – 'searching', 'revealing', 'inspiring', and 'enlightening'.

## The Searching Spirit (vv. 10 and 11)

Notice in passing that the verb shows that the Holy Spirit is personal. For only persons with minds can engage in search or research.

Paul now uses two fascinating pictures, in order to indicate the Holy Spirit's unique qualifications in the work of revelation.

### He searches all things, even the deep things of God (v.10)

The verb (*eraunao*, to 'investigate') is the same word which Jesus applied to Jews who searched or diligently studied the Scriptures (John 5:39). Moulton and Milligan quote a third century papyrus in which 'searchers' seem to be customs officials who rummage about in one's baggage! Further, 'the deep things of God' became a favourite expression of Gnostic heretics and (if this is not an anachronism) Paul may have borrowed it from their vocabulary. Anyway, the Holy Spirit is depicted as a restlessly inquisitive research worker, even a deep-sea diver, seeking to fathom the deepest depths of the being of Almighty God. The Holy Spirit is God exploring the infinity of God.

### He knows the thoughts of God (v.11)

The second model Paul uses seems to be taken from our own

human self-understanding. 'For who among men knows the thoughts of a man, except the man's spirit within him?' (v.11). The word 'thoughts' is literally 'things', a human being's things, perhaps what we would call our 'humanness'. An ant cannot possibly conceive what it is like to be a human being. Nor can a frog or rabbit or even the most intelligent ape or chimpanzee. Nor even can one human being fully understand another. How often, especially in adolescence, we complain 'nobody understands me'. It is true. Nobody understands me except myself, and even my understanding of myself is limited.

Yet this concept of human self-understanding, self-consciousness or self-awareness Paul applies to the Holy Spirit. 'In the same way no-one knows the thoughts of God except the Spirit of God' (v.11b). The Holy Spirit is almost likened to the divine self-understanding or self-consciousness. Just as nobody can understand a human being except that human being himself or herself, so nobody can understand God except God himself. We sometimes sing 'God only knows the love of God'. Similarly, we could say that 'God only knows the wisdom of God or the being of God'. Only God knows God.

So then the Holy Spirit searches the depths of God and the Holy Spirit knows the things of God. He has a unique understanding of God, shared by nobody else. The question is: what has he done with what he has searched out and come to know? The answer is that he has done what only he is competent to do; he has revealed it. The searching Spirit became the revealing Spirit.

## The Revealing Spirit

What the Holy Spirit alone has come to know he alone has made known. This has already been stated in v.10: 'God has revealed it to us (apostles) by his Spirit'. Now Paul elaborates this in v.12: 'We (the same apostolic 'we', the plural of apostolic authority) have not received the spirit of the world, but the Spirit who is from God (namely the searching, knowing Spirit), that we may understand what God has freely given us'.

This indicates that the apostles had received two separate but related gifts from God. First they had received God's free salvation ('what God has freely given us'). Secondly, they had received God's Spirit to enable them to understand the salvation he had freely given to them.

Paul himself is perhaps the best example of this double process. His letters give us a superb exposition of the gospel of grace, how God sent his Son to die for sinners like us, how he raised him from the dead to demonstrate that he had not died in vain, and how we (by faith inwardly, and by baptism outwardly) may become one with Christ in his death and resurrection. But how did Paul know all this? How could he make such a comprehensive statement of salvation? First because he had himself received it, but secondly because he had also received the Holy Spirit to interpret his own experience to him. Thus the searching Spirit became the revealing Spirit. This brings us to stage three.

**The Inspiring Spirit**

Verse 13a: 'This is what we speak'. Or (RSV) 'we impart this', namely this understanding which we have been given.

We notice at once that v.12 speaks of what 'we have received', while v.13 speaks of what we 'impart'. For the apostles imparted to others the understanding which they had themselves received. The searching Spirit, who had revealed God's plan of salvation to the apostles, went on to communicate it through them to others. Just as the Spirit did not keep his researches to himself, but revealed them to the apostles, so the apostles did not keep his revelation to themselves, but imparted it to others. They understood that they were trustees of God's revelation. They delivered to others what they had themselves received.

How did they do so? The answer is given in v.13, namely 'not in words taught us by human wisdom, but in words taught by the Spirit'. We note this further reference to the Holy Spirit, this time as the inspiring Spirit, who gave the apostles the words to speak.

V.13 is an unambiguous claim (on the part of the apostle Paul) to verbal inspiration, namely that the very words in which the apostles expressed their message had been taught them by the Holy Spirit.

I strongly suspect that the reason why the doctrine of verbal inspiration is unpopular is that it is misunderstood. Let me make four statements about it, three negative and one positive.

**a.** Verbal inspiration does not mean that 'every word of the Bible is literally true'. No. The authors use many different literary genres, each of which must be interpreted according to its own rules, history as history, poetry as poetry etc. What is inspired is the natural sense of the words, according to each author's intention, whether this is literary or figurative.

**b.** Verbal inspiration does not mean verbal dictation. Muslims believe that Allah dictated (through the medium of the angel Gabriel) the words of the Koran in Arabic to Mohamed; but Christians believe that the biblical authors were persons and not recording machines. They were not merely taking down divine dictation. They were in full possession of their faculties, even while the Holy Spirit was communicating his words through them.

**c.** Verbal inspiration does not mean that every sentence of the Bible is God's Word, even in isolation from its context. No, the Bible is 'without error in all that it affirms' (Lausanne Covenant). But not everything contained in the Bible is affirmed by the Bible. For example, those long and tedious speeches by Job's comforters were erroneous. Their thesis was that Job was being punished for his personal sin. But they were mistaken. In the last chapter God says twice to them 'you have not spoken of me what is right'. So we cannot quote any sentence from their speeches as God's words. No. Their words were included in order to be contradicted, not in order to be endorsed. The inspired Word of God is what is being affirmed, whether as instruction, command or promise.

**d.** Verbal inspiration means rather that what the Holy Spirit spoke through the human authors, understood according to the plain natural meaning of the words used, and in its context, is true and without error.

There is no need to be embarrassed, ashamed or afraid of this Christian belief. It is eminently reasonable because words are the building blocks of sentences, and so of speech. Words matter! It is impossible to convey a precise message without choosing precise words, as all preachers and lecturers know, and as anybody knows who has needed to send a cable, with only twelve words or so in which to frame the message.

'These glorious things – words – are man's right alone... Without words we should know no more or each other's hearts and thoughts than the dog knows of his fellow-dog... for, if you will consider, you always think to yourself in *words*, though you do not speak them aloud; and without them all our thoughts would be mere blind longings, feelings which we could not understand ourselves...' (Charles Kingsley).

This, then, is the apostolic claim. It is that the same Holy Spirit of God, who searches the deep things of God and knows the thoughts of God, and who revealed his findings to the apostles, went on to communicate them to others through the apostles in words which he gave them. He spoke his words through their words, so that their words were simultaneously his. This is the double authorship of the Bible, already mentioned, and is also the meaning of 'inspiration'.

This brings us to the fourth stage of the Holy Spirit's work as agent of divine revelation.

### The Enlightening Spirit (13b-16)

How are we to think about the people who read the apostles' letters? Were they left to themselves to interpret them as best they could? No. The very same Holy Spirit, who was active in those who wrote the apostles' letters, was (and still is) also active in those who read them. Thus the Holy Spirit was working at both ends, inspiring the apostles and enlightening their readers.

This is already implied at the end of v.13. It is a complicated, even enigmatic, phrase which has been variously interpreted. But I think the RSV is correct in rendering the words 'interpreting spiritual truths to those who possess the Spirit'. In other words, possession of the Spirit was not limited to the biblical authors. Certainly his work of inspiration was unique; we must not claim to be inspired as they were. But to this he added his work of illumination or interpretation. The words 'revelation' and 'inspiration' describe the objective process by which God taught the biblical authors; the word 'illumination' describes the Holy Spirit's *subjective* work of enlightening our minds to understand what the apostles wrote.

Verses 14 and 15 elaborate this truth, and are in stark contrast to each other. V.14 begins with a reference to 'the person without the Spirit', that is, the unregenerate person. V.15 begins with a reference to 'the spiritual person', that is, the Christian, the possessor of the Holy Spirit. For the indwelling of the Spirit is the distinguishing mark of the true Christian (Romans 8:9).

But what difference does it make whether we have the Spirit or not? It makes all the difference in the world!

According to v.14 the person without the Spirit does not receive the things of the Spirit; they are foolishness to him or her; he or she is not able to understand them because they are spiritually discerned. According to v.15 the person with the Holy Spirit, the Christian, 'makes judgments about all things', literally, 'discerns all things'. Not of course that he or she becomes omniscient or infallible, but the things to which he or she was previously blind now begin to make sense.

We now understand what we had not understood before, even though we ourselves are not understood, or literally are 'discerned by no-one'. We remain an enigma to others, because of the inner secret of our spiritual life of which they know nothing. This is not surprising (v.16) because nobody knows the mind of the Lord or can instruct him. And since they cannot understand the mind of Christ, they cannot understand our mind either, who dare to say (because the Spirit enlightens us) 'we have the mind of Christ'.

All this is common Christian experience. For example, William Grimshaw, an eighteenth century evangelical leader in England, wrote after his conversion: 'If God had drawn up his Bible to heaven, and sent him down another, it could not have been newer to him'. He found that it was a different book.

I think I will allow myself a digression at this point, in the form of a question: if the Holy Spirit is the enlightening Spirit, why do we evangelical people still disagree with one another?

My general answer is that we actually agree a great deal more than we disagree. In addition, we would agree even more if we fulfilled the following five conditions.

First, we must accept the supreme authority of Scripture. That is, the big and painful differences are between the reformed and the unreformed churches. Among the reformed churches which accept the supreme authority of Scripture, we are perhaps 90% agreed.

Secondly, we must remember that the chief purpose of Scripture is to bear witness to Christ as Saviour. In this central matter Scripture is perspicuous or plain. Those matters in which Scripture is not clear should be regarded as *adiaphora*, 'matters indifferent', because they are not equally central or important.

Thirdly, we must apply sound principles of interpretation. People sometimes say 'you can make Scripture teach anything you like'. Nowadays I always respond 'you are right, you can – if you are unscrupulous enough!' But if we are scrupulous in our use of proper hermeneutical principles, we will find that far from our controlling Scripture, Scripture controls us. In particular, we need to look for the original sense (according to the author's intention) and for the natural sense (whether this is literal or figurative).

Fourthly, we must study Scripture together, especially in cross-cultural situations, since it is only 'with all the saints' that we shall be able to grasp the dimensions of the love of Christ (Ephesians 3:18).

Fifthly, we must come to the text with a humble and reverent mind. We have to be ready for God to break through our cultural defences, in order to challenge and change us. For if we come to Scripture with our minds made up, and closed, all we will hear from it is what we want to hear, namely the soothing echoes of our own cultural prejudices.

The spiritual discernment which the Holy Spirit promises is not given in defiance of these five conditions; it presupposes them.

I recapitulate. We have considered the role of the Holy Spirit in four stages – searching, revealing, inspiring and enlightening. These are the four stages of his teaching ministry. First he searches the depths of God and knows the thoughts of God. Secondly, he has revealed his findings to the apostles. Thirdly, he has communicated these things through the apostles to others, and has done so in words chosen by him. Fourthly, he enlightens the minds of the readers to discern what he revealed to and through the apostles, and he continues the work of illumination today.

## Conclusion

In conclusion, all this belongs to the ministry of the Holy Spirit as the Spirit of truth. He is also the Spirit of holiness, power and love, but let us honour him as the Spirit of truth as well.

In particular, authentic Christian leadership is impossible without a humble and reverent submission to the authority of Scripture, and an equally humble and reverent dependence on the Holy Spirit. Christian leaders learn to keep in balance the Word of God and the Spirit of God.

Charles Simeon of Cambridge, near the beginning of the last century used to take a sundial as his illustration. If we consult a sundial on a dull day, we cannot tell the time; the dial has no message. But let the sun break through the clouds, and immediately the dial will speak. Just so, if we read Scripture on a dull day, on which we are estranged from God, it has no message for us. But let the light of the Spirit shine on the printed page, and at once the text speaks to us.

# 5. Continuing in the Word (2 Timothy 3:14-17)

Our text is Paul's appeal to Timothy at the end of his life, namely 2 Timothy 3 vv.14-17.

It is important to interpret this text in the light of its context, Paul's appeal in relation to the kind of society which he has described. The chapter begins: 'But mark this: There will be terrible times in the last days'. By these 'last days' the apostle was not referring to some future epoch, but to his own times. We know this because he adds in v.5 the instruction 'Have nothing to do with them'. But how could Timothy avoid such people if they had not even been born? No, 'the last days' were Timothy's days. They are also our days. For the last days began with Jesus Christ; he ushered them in. The last days are the whole period which elapses between his first and second comings.

So what are the characteristics of 'the last days'? Three stand out.

The first is misdirected love, or preoccupation with self. Among the nineteen characteristics of the last days, which Paul mentions in vv. 2-4, six have to do with love. 'People will be lovers of self, lovers of money, lovers of pleasure, instead of lovers of good and lovers of God.' In fact they will be 'without love' (v.3), that is, without authentic love. Is this not true of our times? Self-love, covetousness, hedonism and materialism are rife. The human potential movement seems to have taken over, and people are in love with, even infatuated with, themselves. Certainly the New Age movement has jumped on to this bandwagon. The patron saint of the end of the twentieth century seems to be Narcissus. Self-love has displaced love for God and love for the neighbour.

The second characteristic of these days is empty religion: 'having a form of godliness but denying its power' (v.5). It may seem extraordinary that people characterized by self-love should also be religious. But it is easily possible to be both religious and respectable without being Christian.

In fact, no book ever written is more scathing of empty religion than the Bible. Jesus Christ was more critical of religion even than Marx. Indeed, 'religion' (that is, outward show without inward reality) is one of the greatest enemies of the gospel. Nominal Christianity can inoculate people against real Christianity. And religion can turn people away from Christ.

The third characteristic of these last days is the cult of an open mind. Paul writes of those who are 'always learning but never able to acknowledge the truth' (v.7). Similarly, they 'will not put up with sound doctrine' but instead, 'to suit their own desires, they will gather around them a great number of teachers to say what their itching ears want to hear' (4:3). These are people who sit on the fence and refuse to come down on either side. As is sometimes said, they have nailed their colours to the fence. Tolerance is their watchword. They want to keep an open mind on every issue, and avoid definite convictions. They cannot endure what C S Lewis called 'the tyrannous noon of revelation'; they much prefer the murky twilight of free thought. They forget G K Chesterton's bon mot 'the purpose of opening the mind, as of opening the mouth, is to shut it again on something solid'. Indeed, such people's minds are so open that there is no keeping anything in or out of them.

Here then are three characteristics of Timothy's times, which are characteristic of ours also, and which Scripture trenchantly criticizes. Paul implies that we are (1) to love God and our neighbour, and not misdirect love to ourselves, (2) value the reality and power of religion above its outward forms, and (3) submit humbly to God's revelation and not cultivate a wishy washy agnosticism.

Thus Paul calls Timothy to be different from the world around him. 'But as for you' (v.14), he writes, 'continue in what you have learned and have become convinced of, because you know those from whom you learned it', namely his mother on the one hand and the apostle on the other.

In this passage Paul tells Timothy three truths about the Bible, referring of course in the first place to the Old Testament.

**The Bible Points to Christ**

'From infancy you have known the holy Scriptures, which are able to make you wise for salvation through faith in Christ Jesus' (v.15). Both parts of this statement are significant.

Take first the expression 'wise for salvation'. It indicates that Scripture has an essentially practical purpose, in fact a saving purpose. It is more a guide book than a text book, more a book of salvation than a book of science.

This is not to say that the biblical and the scientific accounts of things are in conflict with each other, but rather that they are complementary to each other. For example, when Jesus said that God 'clothes the lilies of the field', he was not contradicting the mysteries of photosynthesis, but giving an alternative account of plant life, poetic rather than scientific.

The primary purpose of Scripture is not to tell us what we could discover ourselves by empirical investigation, but to reveal truths which we could never discover by the scientific method. Scripture tells us the way of salvation through Christ, that he died for our sins, that he rose again and lives, and that he sent his Spirit.

The second phrase is 'through faith in Christ'. That is, because the Bible is a guide to salvation, it focusses on Christ who came to save. This is true of every part of Scripture. The law shows us our need of Christ because we disobey it, and it condemns us. The sacrifices point forward to the supreme sacrifice of Christ, the lamb of God, whose blood was shed for our redemption. The prophets tell of the coming Messiah, who would first suffer and die, and then rise and reign. The kings foreshadow, however imperfectly, the perfect kingdom of God, which would be a kingdom of righteousness and peace, which would extend throughout the world and last forever. The Gospels tell the story of Jesus' birth and life, words and works, death and resurrection. The Acts tell of what he 'continued' to do and to teach through the apostles. The Letters unfold the full glory of his person and work. The Revelation portrays him walking among the churches on earth, sharing the throne of God in heaven, and coming to save, to judge and to reign.

The reason why Christians love the Bible is that it speaks to us of Christ. We are not bibliolaters, as our critics sometimes describe us; we do not worship the Bible. But we worship Christ, and the Bible points us to him.

I dare say that there is among us a young man who is in love. Probably you carry with you a photograph of your girl friend. Every now and then, when nobody is looking, you may even take her photograph out and give it a surreptitious kiss. But kissing a photo is a poor substitute for the real thing! Yet you love her picture because it speaks to you of her. Just so, we love the Bible because it speaks to us of Christ.

Therefore, whenever we read the Bible, we look for Christ. In former days people put it like this. Just as in England, all roads lead to its capital, London, and wherever you are, every path or track linking on to others, will ultimately bring you to London, so in the Bible, all verses lead to Christ, and wherever you are, every verse linking on to others will ultimately bring you to Christ.

## The Bible Comes from God

Verse 15 states that 'all Scripture is given by inspiration of God' or literally (NIV) 'is God-breathed'. That is, it is the Word of God, breathed out of the mouth of God.

Moreover, this is true of 'all Scripture'. Writing in the middle of the first century, Paul was of course referring to the Old Testament. Yet, with the benefit of hindsight, we may include the New Testament. For the apostolic witness of the New Testament stands alongside the prophetic witness of the Old Testament, as having the same overall divine purpose. Both bear witness to Christ, the Old Testament looking forward to him and the New Testament looking back to him. Together they constitute a single testimony to the mighty acts of God for the salvation of his people.

The New English Bible renders v.15 differently, namely that 'every inspired Scripture is useful ...'. This implies that, although every inspired Scripture is useful, other Scriptures are not in-spired and therefore not useful. But this rendering is unaccept-able and incorrect. For one thing, the very notion of 'uninspired Scripture' is a contradiction in terms, since 'Scripture' means precisely 'inspired writing'. For another, NEB quite unwarrant-ably omits the word *kai* ('and' or 'also'). Yet Paul is making two statements, not one. He is not saying that 'every inspired Scrip-ture is profitable' but that 'every Scripture is inspired and (there-fore) useful'.

We return now to the adjective 'God-breathed'. Of course this is not literal; it is figurative. For God is spirit and therefore has no body. And because he has no body, he has no mouth and no breath. Nevertheless, human speech remains an illuminating model or metaphor of God's communication. It is by our words, by talking to one another, that we come to know one another. Just so, God has made himself known by talking to us. He has breathed words out of his mouth. He has spoken his mind in words.

There is another point we need to consider about the God-breathed nature of Scripture. It is that when God spoke, he did not shout culture-free maxims out of a clear blue sky. Nor did he write some documents and leave them around for people to find (as Joseph Smith is said to have discovered those golden plates). No, he humbled himself to speak through the human authors in their languages (classical Hebrew and *koine* Greek) and in their cultures (those of the Ancient Near East, Palestinian Judaism and the Graeco-Roman world). No word of God was spoken in a cultural vacuum. Every word of God was spoken in a cultural context.

So we are back with the double authorship of Scripture. On the one hand, 'the mouth of the Lord has spoken'. On the other, God spoke through the mouth of his holy prophets'. So out of whose mouth did Scripture come? Was it God-breathed, spoken by the mouth of God? Yes. But was it also breathed and spoken by the mouth of human beings? Yes. Scripture is both the Word of God and the words of men. We must keep the two together, and maintain the integrity of each.

Theologians both ancient and modern, both Catholic and Protestant, have drawn an analogy between Christ and Scripture. Just as in the person of Christ (who is both God and man), we must neither affirm his deity in such a way as to deny his humanity, nor affirm his humanity in such a way as to deny his deity, but affirm both equally, refusing to allow either to contradict the other, so in the Bible we must neither affirm that it is the Word of God in such a way as to deny that it is also the words of men, nor affirm that it is the words of men in such a way as to deny that it is the Word of God, but affirm both equally, refusing to allow either to contradict the other.

### The Bible is Useful to Us

'All Scripture is God-breathed and is useful ...' (v.16, (NIV). Indeed, it is useful to us precisely because it comes from God and points to Christ. It does more than point to Christ. It is useful 'for teaching, rebuking, correcting and training in righteousness'. Here are two antitheses about Scripture. It teaches truth and corrects error; it rebukes evil and trains in righteousness. That is, it relates to both doctrine (truth and error) and ethics (good and evil). Scripture is the essential foundation both of what we believe and of how we behave. In consequence, 'the man of God', or the woman of God, may become a mature person, ' thoroughly equipped for every good work' (v.17).

There is no short cut in this process of becoming the mature men and women God wants us to be. There is only the hard slog of committed discipleship, only the daily, determined discipline of meeting him in Scripture meditation and prayer.

## Conclusion

We have considered Paul's three truths about Scripture, which indicate its great importance. It points to Christ; it comes from God; it is useful for us. How then can we possibly neglect this precious book? If we want to know Christ better, hear what God has to say to us, or grow into maturity, the Bible is essential.

The climax of Paul's exhortation to Timothy is very poignant. Already two or three years previously, he described himself to Philemon as 'an old man'. Now he declares that he has fought the good fight, finished the race and kept the faith (4:7). He is probably in the Mamertine prison in Rome, a dreadful underground dungeon, with only a hole in the ceiling for light and air. He is not expecting to be released from this dismal confinement. Already with his mind's eye he can see the flash of the executioner's sword, and beyond death he sees Jesus, the righteous Judge, ready to award him the crown of righteousness. In other words, his ministry is almost at an end. His preoccupation is with what will happen to the gospel after he has been removed from earth. Hence his exhortation to Timothy to stand his ground against the godless self-centredness of the surrounding culture.

I hope it is not presumptuous, or too personal, for me to apply his words to myself. I am now over seventy years old. I have had my statutory 'three score years and ten'. I am naturally not expecting to live much longer. Any day now my summons may come. So I ask myself: 'Where are the Timothys of the end of the twentieth century, the young men and women who are determined to stand firm against the prevailing winds of fashion and refuse to compromise?' I pray that many may be found among you.

# The Holy Spirit in Word and Works

## A Study in John Chapters 14 to 16

*Vinay Samuel*

### Introduction

In chapters 14 to 16 of John's Gospel the key theme is the work of the Holy Spirit in relation to an unbelieving and hostile world and in relation to the disciples of Jesus.

The Holy Spirit is described as Counsellor (14:16,26; 15:26) and the Spirit of Truth (14:17, 15:26, 16:13). The stress is on the Holy Spirit's work as the Spirit of Truth. The Holy Spirit's work in relation to the world is to convince and judge the world of its guilt in relation to Christ. The Spirit does this as the prosecuting Spirit of Truth. In relation to the disciples, the Spirit is the comforter who will not leave them orphaned but is pre-eminently the Spirit of Truth who leads them into all truth.

The Spirit's work is to confirm, interpret and build on the words of Jesus. The teaching of Jesus becomes the text of the Holy Spirit.

There is also a recognition of the role of the Holy Spirit in enabling the disciples to perform "greater things" than Jesus. The Gift of the Spirit will enable the disciples to do miracles. The study of the passage will highlight the emphasis of the Gospel writer in relating the work of the Holy Spirit to word and works.

## The Spirit of Truth

The Spirit's relation to truth became important in the context which the Fourth Gospel was addressing. It was a context of plurality of religious claims. While a metaphysical oneness of truth was seen as self-evident, no particular religious tradition, narrative or dogma was accepted as universally applicable unless it was promoted through military power. Such a context of competing truth claims and bias towards relativizing any such claims is addressed by the Gospel writer with the teaching of Jesus concerning the role of the Holy Spirit as the Spirit of Truth.

Human society and culture have no place for truth as the Bible defines it. In the Hindu-Buddhist culture in which I have lived you do not question the content of any belief against a standard of truth. You do not attempt to reveal the truth behind any myth or religious narrative. You accept them as they are and where necessary point to other truths both to relativize any claim to universal truth by one, and also to draw out the common ground of all religious narrative. Such a view of truth will spread with Modernity and the Market. Most truths will be accommodated, diluted and distorted. There will hardly be room for a truth which applies to all people and is above all contexts.

## Law Suit of Cosmic Dimensions

The passage in chapter 16 deals with the work of the Holy Spirit in a world which is hostile to Christ's disciples and which rejects the truth of Jesus' teaching. The Holy Spirit is a Counsellor, an Advocate and the Spirit of Truth. The Spirit is described as engaged in a law suit of cosmic dimensions (16:8). Earlier the Gospel focuses on Jesus' legal battle with an unbelieving world "this is the verdict: Light has come into the world but men loved darkness instead of light..." (3:19). Jesus is described as having come to judge the world (9:39). The Father has entrusted judgment to the Son (5:22). The battle is not only with the world in general but is also specifically with the unbelieving Jews (8:42-58). Jesus reveals the unbelieving Jews' origins in the devil, the father of lies as evidenced in their inability to recognize truth let alone understand and accept it. The Jews counter by attacking Jesus' origins. He is a Samaritan and is demon-possessed. The law suit shifts to another level in 12:31. The 'ruler of the world' is judged. The law suit now reaches cosmic dimensions.

From Chapter 13 the focus is on the Holy Spirit seen as prosecuting counsel, who argues his case against the world which rejects his teaching. In relation to the unbelieving, Christ-rejecting world, the Spirit takes on the role of the prosecuting attorney out to prove the world's guilt.

The defendant is the world; the cosmos — a moral order in rebellion against God. It is a world which God loves (John 3:16) and considers redeemable. The teaching of John's Gospel pictures the world as without faith, full of hatred and in active rebellion against God. Contemporary cultures are also marked by violence, bitterness and hatred. In many areas of the world violence and hatred are directed at the disciples of Jesus. In the above passage, the main cause for the world's hatred is identified as the fact of the Incarnation. In Jesus God has become visible in the world. He takes the world on. He becomes part of the world and yet remains free from its corruption and sin. The world cannot stand to be reminded of the possibility of truth, grace, goodness and purity in human history. The incarnate Jesus represents that possibility visibly and so by his very presence he judges the world and rejects its assumptions about the nature of truth and goodness. The disciples who represent such a Jesus are understandably the objects of hatred and vilification.

The hatred of the world is principally directed at Jesus as the teaching and life of Jesus contradicts what the world stands for and judges it. The disciples of Christ are not the primary target, though they do enough to earn ridicule and caricature. They become the target as they represent the possibility of universal truth, of goodness, of love for neighbour, of a unity that overcomes human-made barriers and of the reality of the transcendent in the midst of history.

### The Spirit and the World

The Holy Spirit is described as the Spirit of Truth in relation to the world. In essence and action the Spirit is characterized by truth. It is truth about Jesus (John 16:14). It is truth that Jesus is God's truth and grace. The Spirit will testify about Christ to the world. The world *marturesai* (15:26) could be better translated as "will make an accusation" against the world. The work of the Spirit is to expose and identify the sin of the world. This is as visible a work of the Spirit as the Spirit's work in demonstrating the works of God. In 15:26-7, the Spirit's accusation against the world is supported and reinforced by the "witness" of the disciples. Their existence and continuance in faith is part of their "witness" which accuses and judges the world. Their proclamation of the Gospel is the witness they bear. Their unflinching and sacrificial faith announces that in history a people can maintain its identity and character as the people of God. It can resist the attacks and distortions of the world. The Spirit's testimony against the world is integrally linked to the testimony of the people of God. The Spirit's testimony is neither unhistorical or magical. It takes flesh in the people of God.

In 14:17, Jesus teaches that the world cannot accept the Spirit of Truth "as it neither sees him nor knows him." The world sees Jesus, knows him and rejects him. The Spirit is invisible to the world and the world can close itself to the Spirit as it cannot see its reality or relevance. But the witness of the Spirit as seen in the life of the community of God's people is palpably real. It is visible and relevant and cannot be avoided. The world can either accept or reject. It cannot bypass it.

The Spirit judges the world of sin, righteousness and judgment (16:8-11). There are no definite articles for these words. They focus on values and standards operating in the world. The ideologies that shape the world and the system and structures that make it work are the object of the Spirit's judgment. The Spirit exposes the ideas and structures of the world as sinful against the backdrop of a community of Jesus' disciples who live out the teachings of Jesus and uplift him before the world.

## The Spirit of Truth and the Disciples

The Spirit shapes the lives of the disciples through the revealed truth (15:26, 16:13). The Spirit illumines the words of Jesus in the light of the future. The spirit provides the eschatological framework for the words of Jesus. This protects the word from apostasy as the disciples apply the word to their present and it also protects the disciples from spiritual sterility and coldness. The transmission of the truth oi Jesus and the teaching of Jesus through the community of disciples is monitored, corrected and facilitated by the Holy Spirit. The Holy Spirit enables the disciples to apply the words of Jesus to their futures. As the disciples live out their life in the world, the Spirit applies the words of Jesus to their contexts. The words of Jesus become life-giving in the context but never get trapped in a given context as it is the Spirit who directs their application to a context and their transmission into the future.

The Holy Spirit creates the world of the Bible for any context. In the Gospels truth and the words of Jesus are inseparable. Words are not seen as reflecting an eternal reality out there. Such an assumption of absolute truth as beyond all human words and narratives is a philosophical concept not shared by New Testament writers. The Gospel narrative, the biblical narrative itself is regarded as the truth. However that narrative is dynamically related to the Holy Spirit, who not only inspires the writing of scriptures but continues to be related to their usage by the people of God. The Spirit uses the biblical narrative to create a biblical world. This world of biblical narrative becomes for the disciples, the stable, meaning-giving, life-directing world. The Spirit enables biblical narrative to be both applicable to a given context and to maintain its universality and integrity throughout history.

The biblical world is available universally in all cultures and through all history. The common enterprise of the people of God in different cultures is the study of the world of the Bible as we enter it from our particular cultures. Our particular insights demonstrate the power of the biblical world to judge and transform all our particular worlds. Powerful insights and truths invisible to one culture become accessible through disciples from another cultural background.

The Holy Spirit creates the biblical world in the community of Jesus' disciples. Biblical scholars are necessary to reconstruct with integrity the historical biblical world. Pastors and congregations are necessary to create that world in contemporary history. They become the contemporary, contextual theologians. The biblical world which nurtures and empowers a contemporary congregation is a critically important gift we bring to the world.

Our contemporary worlds and cultures, whether they be Hindu, Latin American, Buddhist, Islamic, traditional, modern or post-modern are in a state of continual change. Contextualizing the Gospel or scripture into this world is always a hazardous task. It is necessary to make the Gospel relevant to different contexts and cultures. I would like to suggest an alternate model of making the Gospel relevant to different contexts.

It is time we recognized the dynamic nature of the world of biblical narrative, especially as it is expressed by a community of disciples who recognize the role of the Holy Spirit in making that world dynamic and empowering. It is into such a world of biblical narrative that is drawn from the Bible, shaped by the Holy Spirit and lived out by a community of believers that we must drag our contemporary contexts. They must be brought into that world and evaluated. The values, principles, systems and structures of the world need to be judged within the framework of the world of the Bible which the Spirit creates in the church.

## The Spirit, the Disciples and "Greater Works"

In John 14:12, Jesus teaches the disciples that any disciple who has faith in him can do 'greater things' than the miracles which Jesus had performed before the disciples. Jesus goes on to link the ability of the disciples to do these greater works to the gift of the Holy Spirit to the disciples, following Jesus' return to the Father.

In his conversation with Philip, Jesus appeals to his teaching as the evidence of his relationship with the Father. The appeal to Jesus' miracles as confirming his oneness with the Father is seen as secondary: "at least believe on the evidence of the miracles themselves" (14:11). For Jesus, the disciples' convictions were better founded on faith in the teaching of Jesus rather than the evidence of the works of Jesus.

Therefore, while the passage goes on to confirm that the gift of the Holy Spirit will enable the disciples to perform great miracles, the Holy Spirit's description as the Spirit of Truth is stressed. The world rejects the Spirit because it cannot accept the truth the Spirit brings and demonstrates. The Holy Spirit is the Teacher who teaches truth to the disciples (14:26, 16:13). It is this truth which is their resource in the world and their weapon against an unbelieving world. The disciples must be empowered by the truth which the Spirit of Truth brings and witness to that truth. The works they will perform will not be the principal weapon the Spirit uses against the world. The works they perform are to strengthen their own faith and confirm the truth of Jesus to them.

The miracles of Jesus in John's Gospel are signs of his identity as the Son of God. They announce that Jesus is God become flesh. In John the disciples' works are not given that role. It is the love which the disciples have for one another that is offered to the world as a testimony (15:11,17; 17:23).

It is possible that John's Gospel does not stress the works of the Holy Spirit through the disciples in relation to the world as it depicts the world as cynical and full of hatred of anything that comes from Jesus. The world shaped by its rejection of Christ will not be impressed with works alone. It is obvious that in John's Gospel the stress is on the Spirit's use of truth, the truth about Jesus, the truth lived out by the disciples against an unbelieving world.

### Conclusion

The above study of the relation between the work of the Holy Spirit to the words of Jesus and the works of the disciples highlights the need for a recovery of the stress on the Johannine teaching of the Spirit of Truth for the contemporary church. The Spirit's creation of the world of biblical narrative in the community life of the disciples as the evidence the Spirit uses to convince, convict and convert the world needs to be accepted and lived out in our contemporary worlds and cultures.

# Canterbury Rap

IN THE BEGINNING WAS THE WORD

God spoke his Word through
    Abraham and Moses,
    Deborah and Hannah,
    Samuel and David,
    Isaiah, Zechariah.

IT IS WRITTEN.     IT IS WRITTEN.

AND THE WORD BECAME FLESH.

God spoke his Word through
    Mary and Elizabeth,
    Simeon and Anna,
    Peter and Paul,
    Matthew and Johanna.

IT IS WRITTEN.     IT IS WRITTEN.

God speaks his Word in
    Urdu and Tamil,
    Xhosa and Hausa,
    Spanish and English,
    Mandarin and Maori.

IT IS READ.     IT IS READ.

IN THE BEGINNING WAS THE WORD.

AND THE WORD BECAME FLESH.

IT IS WRITTEN.     IT IS READ.

IT IS OLD.     IT IS NEW.

IT IS GOD'S.     IT IS TRUE.

## Notes

1. This was written by Graham Kings at the EFAC International Consultation on "the Anglican Communion and Scripture" at Canterbury July 1993. Copyright: Graham Kings, Westminster College, Cambridge, UK. It may be used with acknowledgement and notification.

2. The Congregation recites the lines in capitals.

3. The rhythmic percussion beat is "Ostinato".

There are four bars of introductory beat before the first line; three bars after the first line; there is no gap at all between the end of the verse and the chorus "It is written/read"; one bar between the first and second "It is written/read"; three bars after "And the Word became flesh" (note the short gap between word/became and became/flesh so the stress is on each of those three words); one bar between "It is read" and "In the beginning ..."; one bar after "In the beginning ..."; one bar after "and the Word became flesh"; the next two lines have no gaps in or between the lines and can be divided left and right sides of the congregation (left saying "it is written" and "it is old" etc). The final line is recited all together.

# PART II
# THEOLOGICAL STUDIES

# Scripture Mission and Evangelism

*Cyril C Okorocha*

## Introduction

The question of the relationship between Scripture and Mission and Evangelism is like the question of the relationship between the chicken and the egg: which one produces the other? If for a moment we put mission and evangelism together as the mission of the Church, the question then becomes a question into the relationship between the Scripture, or more precisely, the Bible, and the mission of the Church. There are those who hold that the Scriptures of the New Testament would not exist without the community of faith that compiled them. Others disagree. But the issue is better seen as masterly illustration of the phenomena of mutuality and interdependence. That is, the Church came about through the proclamation of the Word from God as Abram was called by God (Gen. 12). According to Paul, that calling constituted the preaching of the Gospel to Abram (Gal. 3:8). The faith which Abram exercised was as a result of his having heard the word from God. This word from God, both Paul and Peter argue, is the source of saving faith (Rom. 10:17) and the means of rebirth (1 Pet. 1:23) as well as the instrument of liberation or freedom (John 8:32) and sanctification for those who believe (John 17:17).

However, the story of Abraham's response and the consequence of that response to the Word from God is also Scripture or the word about God and God's dealings with humankind.

Similarly, the story of the various responses and activities of those who received the word of God and their encounter with the world as a result of that word, is also Scripture (see Luke 1:1-3; Acts 1:1-3; Heb. chaps. 11-12). Peter classifies Paul's writings as Scripture. Thus, those who believe Scripture, are said to be Scripture people or Evangelicals. Put more radically, John Stott once defined Evangelicals as Bible people: they believe the Bible; they live by the Bible and they proclaim the message of the Bible. If we hear from God, our life is transformed and we are impelled by the dynamism encapsulated in that word to go on telling the story that transformed our own lives.

Scripture and mission are inseparable. The word from God turns those who receive it into a missionary people. For example, God called Abram not to a solitary and contemplative life, but to dynamic, deviant and prophetic life with a definite purpose: "Go from your people to a land that I will show you ... your children will be blessed and ... all the nations of the earth will be blessed through your seed ..." (Gen 12:1-4). In short, the Word of God comes to humankind with or as an apostolic mandate. In other words, the proof of having heard the word on the part of any person or group is their apostolicity. There is a sense of having a special mandate and a special message which must be delivered with a sense of urgency as a matter of life and death. "I will bless those who bless you and through you all the families of earth will bless themselves."

So Abram responded to the call to go. The immediate consequence was that his identity, later to be epitomised in his new name Abraham, was bound up with this response, this new mission. In relation to the Church, I have elsewhere[1] argued that the Church exists for mission: that a Church that does not engage seriously in mission loses its identity and apostolicity and soon degenerates into a mission field for other religions. In short, the Christianness of any people is measured in terms of their evangelistic missionary zeal. We are a people with a message and a mandate. Paul could cry out "woe to me if I do not preach the Gospel" (1 Cor. 9:16).

Thus our identity is bound up with our response to this Word from God, the Scriptures. We shall now examine ways in which that same word shapes our identity and determines our destiny as the Church of God and that of the world to which we have been called to declare the word from God, the message of Scripture.

## The Word from God and the Mission of the Church

*Scripture tells us the meaning of mission and evangelism*

Scripture defines the meaning of the people of God as a people called out with a purpose or mission: that of reaching the rest of humanity with the word of or from God. That word is Good News. Scripture makes no distinction between mission and evangelism; or between evangelism as proclamation and social action as practical application of the message proclaimed. To evangelize means to bring Good News. Those who embody that Good News are said to be a people with a mission. So the mission of those who are bringing the Good News is evangelizing, that is their business. In practical terms: why is the Church here? The Church is a community of people with a special mission. What is that mission? It is to bring Good News — to evangelize. Therefore, as I have discussed elsewhere, the raison d'être of the Church in the world is to bring Good News — to evangelize.[2] Brunner argued that as fire exists by burning, so the Church exists through mission/evangelism. As fire is fire and only so, because and only if it burns, so also the Church: the Church is Church only if it is evangelizing, i.e., engaged in bringing the Good News.

Because Scripture places no dichotomy between mission and social action or between evangelism as proclaimed and mission as dynamic presence, this mission of the Church must therefore be viewed as a holistic venture in which the people of God unite all the resources at their disposal, material and spiritual, in a relentless effort to bring God's Good News to all persons in context. Because it is a holistic venture, that mission of the Church in the world involves hazards as well as joyful harvest. But it must include five inseparable aspects, viz proclamation, demonstration, preservation, anticipation and participation in partnership. We declare the Good News, that is the perfect atonement in Christ and thus the possibility of adoption into

God's family, we demonstrate it in our lives in qualitative conduct and by loving deeds; we preserve it in the natural order, i.e., by preserving God's hand in and respecting creation, and God's moral values in human behaviour as revealed in the Word from God, and as we struggle to bring hope into a hopeless and needy world; we involve all of God's people irrespective of ethnicity, gender, race or social class in this great and exciting mission and thus assert God's impartiality and universal love. This is the meaning of mission and evangelism, according to Scripture, the bringing of God's Good News to everyone in context.

### Scripture gives us the mandate

The mandate to evangelise is implicit in the first call and demonstrated in the response and actions of the earliest members of the Church. For example, included in the call to Abram is an encouragement to hope for a universal blessing through him. In short, with his call came a mandate for a global mission and ministry (Gen. 12:1-4). Abraham responded to the call, not alone, but with his wife Sarah and his nephew Lot. He had a masterly combination of the family (including the extended family) or local and the global aspects of mission.

When Peter and John were called, they were promised: "I will make you fishers of men" (humanity) — those who will call humanity to the paths of life and truth. They responded not only by following, but on a different occasion had been instrumental in finding others. Peter took along his younger brother Andrew and so did James who took John (Mark 1:16-20). Andrew was said to have, on another occasion, taken the initiative for pressing Peter into a more permanent commitment to the one whom he had come to believe to be the long expected Messiah: "We have found the Messiah," he said to Peter, bringing him to the Saviour who gave him a new name which encapsulated his new faith and future ministry. Philip responded to the call and inspiration to convince sceptic Nathaniel, at least to give this new teacher a chance before writing him off as an upstart of inconsequential social class (John 1:35-51). Nathaniel became a believer of deep intellectual integrity and conviction as a result.

The 'Great Commission' (Mark 16:15ff & Matt. 28:20ff) is usually regarded as the mandate to evangelize. But our view is that the call to mission is bound up with the call of the people of God into becoming the Church; and that the mandate to mission is writ large on every page of Scripture and bound up with the call, identity, experience and destiny of the people of God. We are the people of God because we proclaim the word about God. Those speaking about Jesus as the Christ were soon nicknamed Christians (Acts 11:26), while in the Gospels, the Lord said that the eschaton which we anticipate must be presaged by the total evangelisation of the world (Matt. 24:14). Right from the call of Abram or even before, (see the case of Noah for example), the story of the people of God is the story of a people with a mission. The call to conversion through God's grace is itself a call to mission. Peter and John argued that it would be total betrayal of reason to fail to stand up to what they had seen and experienced (Acts 4:19, 20; 2 Pet. 3:16-18). The privilege or grace of believing is the mandate to mission. The source of this mandate is not just one or two isolated texts but the whole Bible. Every page of the Bible is about mission. Stott argues thus:

> Without the Bible world evangelization would be not only impossible but actually inconceivable. It is the Bible that lays upon us the responsibility to evangelise the world, gives us a Gospel to proclaim, tells us how to proclaim it, and promises us that it is God's power for salvation to very believer.[3]

An important corollary to our argument so far is that our perceptions of and commitment to our mission as the people of God is dependent on our fidelity to the source of that mandate. In missiological terms, it is our attitude to the Word of God that decides our commitment or otherwise, to the word about God. That is the degree of the Church's commitment to world evangelization at any point in history, is a measure of her commitment to Scripture as the Word from God. Whenever Christians lose their confidence in the Bible as God's Word with divinely inspired authority, they also lose their zeal for and confidence in their faith and in evangelism. History and hard facts of contemporary experience affirm that liberal Churches are the breeding ground for all sorts of confusing heresies and the sign of the dying and dead wood in the spiritual forest. Those who have led the Church into world evangelism and self recovery have always been men and women of clear views and strong yet graceful personal convictions about their own faith (in Christ) and the authority of the Scriptures. When we are sure of our source of authority we can act fearlessly and with conviction. So if we are to call the Church back to serious commitment to world evangelism, then we must help her recover faith and confidence in the Scripture as the Word from God with full divine authority to fulfil the purpose for which it was sent, that of healing humanity and reconciling them to God (Isa. 55:10,11; 2 Cor. 5:18-20).

### Scripture gives us the motive for mission

Why should we evangelize?

David Bosch in his impressive work, *Transforming Mission* outlines a number of wrong motives for mission which *inter alia* include:

a. **The eschatological motive** which is driven by an alarming concern that the 'end is near', and that the Lord's return is dependent upon our completing the evangelisation of the world.[4] The school of thought represented by Ralph Winter et al has mapped out the 10-40 window and is encouraging Churches (of the West) to 'adopt a people group' so as to hasten on the process of world evangelism and thus the Lord's return. There is a constant play on and reinterpretation of the word ethnic (in terms of people or people groups). The argument is that the Lord is not asking us to evangelize or convert the nations but to evangelize – almost in a modern nuclear fashion, 'gospelize', people groups and the Lord will believe that they have been evangelized! He will then return and set up his kingdom for the faithful missionaries and donors!

This hastiness cheapens the Gospel and caricatures the meaning of conversion. This viewpoint necessarily leads to a disinterested attitude to the socio-political immediacy. In Third World countries, nationalist politicians often write off such Churches as agents of the imperialists and their leaders are branded colonialist pawns and national traitors. But, there often arises a completely opposite reaction whereby the nationalists resort to religion and a parody of Christian theology and ideas in the struggle for liberation, identity and equality. The plethora of liberation and ethnic theologies arising from the Third World and including Black theology, Theology of Humanization, etc, bear out this point.

b. **The Church planting motive** is equally misleading in that it tends to drive the missionary to struggle to show their success in the form of tangible results – a new church or churches, 'planted'. Besides, there is a tendency to try to reproduce the home church in all its forms and doctrines. This leads to more denominational rivalries among the missionaries, and ecclesiastical imperialism in relation to the new churches, as the 'baby churches' must be nurtured and controlled by the 'parent church'. When we remember that churches are people, not buildings, the dehumanizing implications of such naivete become more obvious.[5] The Peter Pan syndrome (or 'dependence legacy') that persists in the young churches of the Third World today, may be traced to the hasty 'church planting' mentality of some early Western missionaries. This on the other hand leads to the beggar and cheque book approach to partnership which seems to characterise North-South relationships.

c. **The philanthropic motive** is the most subtle and least easily discernible error. This is the challenge to seek justice in the world, to work to improve the lot of the poor, the less privileged and apparently oppressed. The outcome is often the equation of the kingdom of God with improved society which is achieved by a humanistic *tour de force*. This leads to the amplification of the virtues of the poor without realising that the God of Christian theism has no favourites. He is at once the God of the oppressed, the Saviour of both the oppressed and the oppressor and Judge of all. (The message of repentance must go to the rich and poor alike and all must be called to receive the love of God.) More obnoxious still is the humiliation to which the 'poor' are subjected as their condition in its most grotesque form is orchestrated and publicised in order to enlist support and arouse pity from politicians and donors. This creates the image of a perpetually hungry Africa and Asia. The reactions of Third World politicians and intellectuals to such dehumanization and its counter productive evangelistic effect are too obvious to require further description here.

d. **The social justice motive.** A crucial note of caveat for

missiologists and Church leaders, signalled by this seemingly
noble motive in mission is that it is impossible for the Church of
the crucified man of Nazareth to become a political religion
without losing her identity. In short, while it is true that the
religion of Jesus of Nazareth is not other worldist, it is equally
true that the religion cannot be an ally of humanistic political
forces and ideologies and still remain true to Jesus Christ (John
18:17).[6] "My kingdom is not of this world ..." the dying Saviour
insists. This may sound defeatist like a betrayal of Christians
under totalitarian religiously based states, in Africa and parts of
Latin America for example; or for those under the pressure of
militant Islam, Nigeria for example. The fact remains that the
Kingdom we proclaim is of God and from God, and its final
realisation is essentially futuristic. We wait for a Kingdom to
come "whose builder is God" (Heb 11:10). This does not indicate
other worldism or a negation of the possibility of justice in the
immediacy. Rather it says two things: first that any definition or
pursuit of *Yesa* or *soteria*, God's salvation of humankind, which
if not undergirded by a certain future hope is bound to lead to a
frustrating spiritual *cul de sac* and theological dishonesty. The
Kingdom of God will not be realised through a human process
rooted in a Hegelian dialectic. Even human socio-political systems so based have recently proved their foundations to be fluid,
Soviet Socialism for instance. The Western Monetarist Capitalism is not a reliable alternative model either.[7]

A second implication is that in every biblically sound proclamation of or action for the Kingdom of God is a paradox. A
paradox which Archbishop Carey recently described as a Transforming Vision: suffering and glory in God's world. That is, there
is always an inescapable 'not yet' about the Kingdom we proclaim; a tentativeness which frees us from naivety and gives us
courage to wait and strength to love and forgive our enemies
until it hurts, and to suffer in hope (for example, Martin Luther
King Jr, Desmond Tutu and Mother Theresa).

Scripture, however, tells us that there can be selfish motives
involved in mission, most outstanding among them being the
motive of financial gain. Some people, according to Paul, think
that the commitment to the Gospel or mission is a means to
financial enrichment. Such people fall into the trap of the devil

(1 Tim. 6:8-10) as the love of money is a root to all kinds of evil. Their end is according to their deeds since their god is their appetite (Phil. 3:19). True believers are warned to avoid such persons as their selfishness soon becomes evident in their decadent morality (1 Tim. 6:6-11; 2 Tim. 3:1-9). The prophets whose ministries were economically motivated were stooges of corrupt political ideologies and systems, Amaziah (Amos 7:14 ff) for instance, and blind advocates and supporters of corrupt status quo, Ahab's 400 private prophets, for instance, as contrasted with Micah (2 Chron. 18:21,22).

e. In modern times, it is also possible to add to this list of wrong motives, the private **empire building motive:** those who are bent on extending their image and area of control, sometimes in competition with some other entity which commands world fame. Their ministry is characterised by superficiality and imbalance — usually extremist Biblical liberalism which is often manipulatory both of Scripture and people. Their end is according to their deeds. The tragedies of modern 'tele-evangelists' and cult leaders such as the Revd. Jim Jones of Jones Town, Guyana (1980), the Waco sect and the Children of God are too obvious to require delayed discussion. The point here is that it is not enough to claim to be preaching the Gospel or involved in mission, it is important that the motive is right, biblical and Christo-centric. Scripture gives us a broad sweep of the right motives for mission: These include:

i. A full appreciation of who we are. To know that our calling is to mission means to be involved in mission. To fail to do so will be pejorative to our very existence. To be a Christian is to be a missionary a person with a message. Paul asserts "I am under an obligation .... woe is me if I do not preach the Gospel." Our identity as the people of God is bound up with the Gospel.

ii. It is the very reason why we are called. We are saved to serve. We are here as his witnesses (Isa. 43:6-8) and he saves, sanctifies and empowers us in order that we may bear his goodness to other (Mark 3:13-15; Acts 1:8).

iii. The salvation of others depends on our proclamation "how can they believe in him of whom they have not heard?" "Faith comes from hearing ... the word from/about Christ" (Rom. 10:13-17).

Thus Scripture teaches us not only to love God and seek his glory, but to love our fellow human beings and work for their salvation. Where this altruistic love is lacking as a missionary motive, mission degenerates into a paternalistic venture at worst or a "civilizing mission" at best. In either case, the outcome is often cultural or economic imperialism.

iv. Scripture tells us that the love of Christ must control us (2 Cor. 5:14). Love for the Saviour should motivate us to proclaim him to others. This is our way of showing gratitude to him for first giving himself for us. In the words of C.T. Studd: "If Jesus Christ be God and died for me, then no sacrifice can be too great for me to make for him." Paul would give up everything for "the surpassing glory of knowing and appropriating Christ ... who loved me and gave himself for me" (Phil. 3:8; Gal. 2:20). Cf. "Love so amazing so divine Demands my soul, my life my all."

But does it just 'demand' or does it deserve our all? Is it not true that all we are and have comes from him and whatever we give to God was his in the first instance? (1 Chron. 29:14).

This grateful love for God leads us to seek his glory and that alone is the course of our mission to win his world back to him (cf. John 5:41-44; 14:23-24; Rom. 12:1,2). This grateful love for God makes our obedience to the Great Commission not the motive but the result of our appreciation of his prevenient love for us. Paul says: "It is not I, but the grace of God in me" (1 Cor. 15:10). Some people get into 'mission' as a grudging duty in 'obedience to the Great Commission'. Such people soon burn out. They are full of grudges and bitter complaints against the mission board, the Church, the bishop, anybody, except themselves! But when the love of Christ controls and motivates us, our attitude will be different (see, for example, Acts 5:40-42; Phil. 3:7-11).

### Scripture give us the message for mission and evangelism

That message is the Word from God, enshrined in the infallible Scriptures of the Bible and epitomized in the person, life and ministry of Jesus Christ. In short, Jesus Christ is the message of our evangelism. He is the Good News from God. It is a simple story, but a special story. According to the Lausanne Covenant, evangelism is to

> spread the Good News that Jesus Christ died for our sins, and was raised from the dead according to the Scripture, and that as the reigning Lord he now offers forgiveness of sins and the liberating gift of the Spirit to all who repent and believe in him.

The message we proclaim is the message of Scripture, that is Jesus Christ. This is the way he puts it: "Search the Scriptures .... they speak of me" (John 5:39). In other words, I am the subject and central concern of the Scriptures.

> From Moses and all the prophets, he explained to them the things concerning himself in all the Scriptures (Luke 24:22).

So our message, the word from God which we pass on to humankind for their salvation, is the message about Jesus Christ as revealed in the Bible.

We have no right to alter that message. There is a givenness and sacredness about the Gospel which we neglect or tamper with at our peril (Gal. 1:6-12). It is a historical message which has its roots in the Mosaic tradition and Hebrew history (2 Tim. 1:5) but which transcends that tradition. It is a message of power — the power from God that brings salvation to all who believe (Rom. 1:16) and whoever calls upon the name of the Lord shall be delivered (Joel 2:32ff). It is a message of, from and about, the most supreme authority ever to be conceived: "At the name of Jesus, every knee shall bow" (Phil. 2:9-11); Luke 10:18-20). It is a message of forgiveness through the atoning Blood of Christ. There is a tendency these days for people to preach a bloodless Christianity! But without the cross, there will be no blood and "there is no forgiveness without the shedding of blood."

Nevertheless, the Gospel we proclaim is also the message of deliverance from sin and its power, and from all the power of the devil. The deliverance/liberation and power/authority aspect of the mission of the Church may frighten Western evangelicals, excite some and is subject to abuse.[8] Yet it is very important to

Christians and peoples of the non-Western world: whereas the West views God as an eirenical, and ever so benevolent, Grandfather whose concern is to see to the forgiveness of his erring siblings, and has religious aspirations motivated by guilt and a desire for forgiveness, the over-riding African concern is for power from a mighty God to deliver them from the innumerable factors that vitiate life and indicate death.[9]

But this is not alien to the scriptural understanding of the *Missio Dei*, God's mission in the world, as revealed through the Christ event. As shown already, Jesus Christ is in his person, work, and utterance, the subject and central concern and sum of the message of Scripture. In short, he is the brevarium totium evangeli, the most accurate and most tacit expression of the Gospel in its meaning and message (cf Heb. 1:1-2).

By the same line of thought, the mission of God in this world, epitomized in the Christ event includes, deliverance from the power of darkness (Col. 1:13; 2:14-16); destruction of the works of the devil (1 John 2:8); freedom from poverty, especially spiritual poverty (Matt. 5:3; Isa. 55:1-2); deliverance from fear — especially of death (2 Tim. 1:10; Heb. 2:14-16); liberation from captivity to vice, and other dehumanizing factors so as to usher in, for the believer, a life full of abundance i.e., total wholeness (Luke 4:18ff; Isa. 61:1-3; John 10:10). In short, Scripture presents us with a full Gospel message that implies total salvation which goes beyond mere *aphesis* to include all that *soteria* means including the incorporation of the ancient ideas signified by the Hebrew theme *yesa*.[10]

Viewed in this way, the Gospel we proclaim is not out of touch with contextual realities while maintaining its essential and divine otherness wherein lies its saving power (see 1 Pet. 1:17-23; 2 Tim. 3:15-16; Rom. 1:16). In other words, the mission of the Church is an incarnational experience, slow, painful but sure: a transforming vision which demonstrates its sincerity in word and deed. In practice, the Church becomes God's co-labourer as the go-between-God causes fresh light to shine into a given context making it possible for Christ to become incarnate into that situation, dispelling darkness and ushering in a kingdom of integrity and wholeness (John 1:1-5; 8:12).

## Scripture gives us a model for mission

Scripture not only gives us a message for the mission to which we are called it also models it for us.

First, Scripture shows us that the initiative for mission must always come from the one who has the message. It was God who took the initiative to invite Abram (Gen. 12:1-4). The prophets felt that the privilege of hearing from God carried with it the responsibility of delivering that word consistently and with integrity to those who needed it. The Word from God that came to them was a word for others. But there was a disturbing sense of ought that this privilege placed on them; see for example Ezekiel 33:1-9.

They did not wait to be invited. Yes, there is always a Macedonian call from our fellow Christians to join them in partnership in their local mission, but whoever has heard the Word of God is, by that singular experience a prophet, and a model of that Word. Paul felt under a compulsive sense of ought in view of the mercy he had received from God; "Woe is me if I do not preach the Gospel," he asserted (1 Cor. 9:16), so that "the Grace of God in me is not in vain" (1 Cor. 15:10).

Second, Scripture also makes a distinction between the missionary mandate and the missionary experience. The missionary mandate "go and tell..." came from God to the prophets of the Old Testament; from the risen Christ to the apostles and by implication to the Church; and from the Holy Spirit through the Church at Antioch as a community of faith, faithfully representing the risen Christ in worship and witness, to Paul and Barnabas (see for example Isa. 6:9ff; Amos 7:14-17; Matt. 28:20; Acts 13:2, etc.).

Two missiological axioms stand out here. One such axiom is that implicit in the apostolic mandate is an onus on the part of the missionary to maintain an accountable relationship with the source of that mandate. The Old Testament prophets felt that their very life depended on their delivering the message according to Yahweh's stipulations, no matter how difficult. To fail to do so could be disastrous (for example Balaam, Num. 22:18); Paul made it his aim to be found pleasing to God no matter what that cost him (2 Cor. 9:5), and to keep a clear conscience before God and people (Acts 23:1; 24:16). Hence he lived a life of prayer, but from time to time returned to base to give account of his work (Acts 14:26-28) and of his financial dealings and especially of resources such as gifts of money and other items entrusted to him in the course of that work (see 1 Cor. 16:1-4; 2 Cor. chaps 8-10). The point here is that it is not enough to be right with God, privately, it is important to be seen and known to be in the right. To this group relationship, Paul also added accountability or mutuality, and interdependent relationship with some other key trusted Christians and fellow workers. This was for his own personal spiritual and moral security and assistance in the ministry (see Acts 17:15, 16; 1 Cor. 16:12-14; 2 Tim. 4:11).

The other missiological axiom is that mission is a movement, not of money, necessary as this may appear to the work, or of socio-political power, but of spiritual power from those who have it. This raises the question as to where the Church's power base lies at the moment and therefore, where the missionary movement should be originating from, in view of the current demographic shift in the Church.[11]

However, along with the missionary mandate, Scripture shows that the Christian presence in any locale may be regarded as a missionary experience. Every true Christian is, *ipso facto*, part of this presence in so far as they take their faith seriously. It is an unpremeditated and unplanned powerful influence of the Spirit which accompanies all those who are truly in touch with God. In the cadence of every day life and as they engage in their normal duties and professions, people recognise them as being in possession of a rare quality of life which we all need (Acts 4:13).

In addition to the initiative model, Scripture gives us a pattern for our missionary activity. The import of Acts 1:8 is that mission is dependent upon the power of the Holy Spirit and that power spreads outwards from the place of initial impact with salvific effect. In other words, the mission of the Church begins where the Church is. It is unscriptural to think of the Church's locale as a 'sending base' only and the mission field elsewhere in the far away lands and finally to the ends of the earth. It is naive thinking of a Church's locale only as a 'sending base', and the mission field being elsewhere. Some of the old hymns encourage that line of thought "Far, far away in heathen lands dwelling..." But Scripture encourages us to believe that wherever the Church exists, there is mission.

The third model that Scripture gives us is the nature of mission. The prophets, Jesus and the Apostles appeared to have had three areas of emphasis in their ministry: Teaching in the synagogues. That is, giving the Gospel in its maximum or detailed demand to those who had already heard and experienced its first impact, Preaching in all their villages and cities: this may be taken as introducing the Gospel and proclaiming it with a view to enlisting response to conversion; and Healing. The prophets, Jesus and the apostles healed people's bodies, minds and emotions. They healed family and interpersonal relationships and pointed the way to the healing of society. Scripture asserts that God's justice is perfect and 'horizontal justice'. The poor are not poor just because they are poor. God, as revealed in Scripture, has no grandchildren and does not practice favouritism. He is God of the penitent, Saviour of the importunate and Judge of all — both the oppressed and the oppressor (see John 8:1-11; Matt. 18:21-35).

Scripture also shows that the call to repentance is a central theme in mission and evangelism and that *Missio Dei* is a saving movement rooted in the Christ event, the atonement which includes the blood of Calvary. Thus, in preaching repentance and proclaiming the atonement, Scripture gives us a message of hope. The penitent sinner can be forgiven (Isa. 44:22, 23; Matt. 3:1-12; 4:17; John 3:16-19; 1 John 4:10; Rom. 5:6-11). Sacrifice for sin has been made once and for all (Heb. 10:10-14). That sacrifice is final and sufficient. We cannot bypass the cross else we will be found guilty of preaching another Gospel.

But the message of healing includes the possibility of and call to involvement in social transformation and honest struggle for social justice. However, Scripture seems to suggest that lasting transformation of society is possible only through Holy Spirit transformed people.

### Scripture gives us a pattern of the measure of mission

How much should I forgive my brother: seventy times seven times? Not just seven times, but much more: to the degree to which I would like God to forgive me (Matt. 6:14,15; 18:35). In short, we are to learn to love and to go on sharing God's altruistic *agape*, love, until it hurts. The measure of our love is what Jesus Christ has done for us. Heb. 12:1-5 reminds us of the cloud of witnesses, past and present and gives us the measure and rationale for our love and service, the passion of Christ.

### *Scripture gives us the means or authority for our mission in God's world*

First, Scripture gives us the authority of right of a filial relationship with God. Thus our involvement in the *Missio Dei* is involvement in 'Our Father's business'. There is a saying among African peoples that a stranger does not join a chase after a thief as he might be mistaken for the thief.

This makes the need to be born into the household of faith crucial for all who wish to be involved in *Missio Dei*. John 1:12,13 gives us the authority to, and possibility of, 'divine parenthood' while Acts 19:13-17 warns of the danger implicit in seeking to do God's work as an imposter. Some African peoples say that a sympathizer does not get hysterical with grief at a funeral! Only a close blood relative does. The grief belongs personally to him. Hence, Jesus explained the unmitigated zeal with which he committed himself to his work as doing his Father's business and commanded his disciples to serve similarly: "As my Father has sent me so send I you" (John 20:21-13).

Second, Scripture gives us authority over sin and the sin factor in our lives, so that when we proclaim repentance and forgiveness, we could do so with integrity (Rom. 6:14; 7:25; 8:3; Jer. 31:34).

Third, Scripture gives us authority over fear especially the fear of death (John 4:18; Heb. 2:14-16; 1 Tim. 1:10; 1 Cor. 15:19ff).

Fourth, Scripture shows us that in Christ, we have authority over all the powers of the enemy (Luke 10:18ff; 1 John 4:4; 5:4,5). We appropriate this authority in Christ through prayer. Satan trembles when the weakest saint kneels. This is because "prayer is the power that moves the hand that moves the world to bring salvation down."

Those waiting to engage in the *Missio Dei*, according to Scripture need to be sure of their right of inheritance in Christ through rebirth into the community of faith (Rom. 8:14-17); they need to give themselves to study the Scriptures, the source of their message and mandate (2 Tim. 2:15; 3:15-17); they must spend time in prayer so as to appropriate their authority in Christ over the powers of the enemy. Authority is superior to power. *Missio Dei*, as said already, is not a social or political venture. It is a spiritual warfare. In that battle our weapons are not humanistic: they are "mighty through God" (2 Cor. 10:3-5; Eph. 6:10-18).

## *Scripture sets out the manners or character required of those engaged in mission and evangelism*

The most authenticating factor of the veracity of the Gospel we proclaim is the character of those who proclaim it. Paul lamented that there were those who proclaimed the Gospel but their whole life style was a contradiction of what they proclaimed. Paul agonized over such people whom he described as "enemies of the cross of Christ" (Phil. 3:18). Our Lord warned against the possibility of preaching the Gospel and even experiencing the power of the age to come and still missing out on the final admission into his immediate presence, as a result of living lives that contradicted the message of the Gospel. He described such persons as "workers of iniquity," damnable characters, whose "end shall be according to their deeds" (Matt. 7:20-22; Phil. 3:17, 18).

But Samuel, and later Paul, showed by their own personal examples that those who proclaim such as holy message must live holy lives in all aspects of human endeavour. They are to be free from greed, cheating, dishonesty, moral misdemeanour, etc; in short they are to be persons who are utterly reliable — or "above reproach" (see 1 Sam. 12:2-5; Acts 20:18-21; 1 Tim. 3:2-7).

Papias, the revered elder of the early second century Church at Ephesus, had a dictum which he asked the Churches to use to test the veracity of the innumerable peripatetic preachers (cf. Tele-evangelists of today) that besieged the Churches in those days.

No matter what they claim or preach or what visions they claim to have seen or miracles they claim to have performed, the final test is this: 'do they have the behaviour of the Lord?'

This is the mark of a true prophet and minister of Christ! And how we all need this mark as evangelical Christians in these days of so much counterfeit of everything!

Pope John Paul II in a recent encyclical sounds a similar note:

The call to mission derives, of its nature, the call to holiness. Holiness must be called a fundamental presupposition and an irreplaceable condition for everyone in fulfilling the mission of salvation in the Church. The universal call to holiness is closely linked with the universal call to mission. Every man ... is called to holiness and mission (1991:56).

'Unless I see the mark of the nails' signs of the crucifixion, insisted Thomas, 'I will not believe.' The point here is that people will believe our preaching to the degree they see the authentic Jesus in our lives. That was Paul's strongest point against his critics and opponents and the most authentic sign of his apostolicity in the face of so much opposition. He urged Timothy but "you have followed my life and teaching ... knowing from whom you have learned them." His life was a mirror, an open screen on which all could see and read his sermons. His impeccable personal character and integrity were his greatest treasure and defence (see for example 2 Tim. 3:10-14; Acts 20:29-35). What a challenge to us all.

### Scripture warns us of the minefields of mission and evangelism

Apart from physical dangers and possible violent persecutions, those who engage in *Missio Dei* in a world hostile to God are warned of a number of subtle, but highly potent dangers hidden along their way. Luke 4:1-13 is classic here, especially as it ends with a reminder that the devil did not go on retirement after tempting Jesus in the wilderness; he was lurking around, waiting for another opportunity — a loop hole, an unguarded moment. Peter says he is like a wounded and hungry roaring lion, desperately in search of a prey.

Paul warned those in the ministry to be particularly aware of two serious (but common) dangers among many.

The first is the love of money which he described as a root to all kinds of evil and a source of 'ministerial derailment', including entanglement in political and humanistic power struggle and compromise of one's faith and values. (1 Tim. 6:9,10). The second is sexual immorality, rife in Paul's day but today described as the spiritual cancer of modern Christian leadership. I was at a meeting recently when a speaker gave frightening statistics of Christian leaders — some of them evangelical, who had currently been caught in this tragic web. The shame, the material poverty, the loss of spiritual power, of reputation and alienation and heartache it brings into homes, should be a warning to drive us to heed Paul's injunction.

> 'But you, O servant of God, flee these things'; flee sexual immorality! Rather pursue righteousness, piety, faith, love, patience, meekness. Fight the good fight of faith, lay hold on eternal life to which you are called ... (1 Tim. 6:11,12).

The 'good fight' is to be engaged in *Missio Dei* the proclamation of the whole word to the whole world. This is our calling. Biblical scholarship is inescapable but it must be scholarship that lets loose the truth of the word wherein lies its saving power. The word is a two-edged sword. It is foolish and dangerous to fight over it. It is like a lion.

> The best way to defend it is to let it loose! If only every Christian missionary and evangelist proclaimed the biblical Gospel with faithfulness and sensitivity; and every Christian preacher were a faithful expositor of God's Word! Then God would display his saving power in the world![12]

That same word gives us the authority and the mandate, to be so engaged! It clearly and powerfully outlines the models of the mission and the character of the missionary and warns us of serious dangers and yet assures us of victory and authority through Jesus Christ our Lord.

### Questions for discussion

1. 'The Bible and only the Bible shall be our rule of faith, conduct and action'. Can such a stand be sustained today and what challenges confront those who try to do so?

2. The call to Christian discipleship is *ipso facto* a missionary call. Therefore, 'to be a Christian is to be a missionary'. Discuss.

3. 'I see the dawning of a new missionary age ... an abundant harvest, if all Christians ... and the young Churches in particular, respond with generosity and holiness to the calls and challenges of our time' (Pope John Paul II).

Is there sufficient evidence in Scripture and possibly from Church history,

a. to suggest a pattern of paradigm shifts and possible reversals in the centre of gravity and direction of the Christian missionary movement?

b. to closely link personal (and collective) holiness and Christianness of character of the members of the Church with their effectiveness in mission? Discuss with practical illustrations.

4. 'The missionary zeal and effectiveness of the Church in any age is commensurate with the degree of her conviction about the authority of the Bible' (Stott). Discuss.

5. 'Sexual immorality is the spiritual cancer of modern Christian leadership'. Is this a curse or could there be a cure? What does Scripture say?

## Notes

1. Cyril Okorocha, "The Church Exists for Mission" in *EFAC Bulletin*, 1992.

2. Cyril Okorocha, "The Meaning of Religous Conversion in Africa: its missiological implications" (Geneva, Mission Studies, 1992)

3. John R.W. Stott, "The Bible in World Evangelization" in Winter R. *et al.* (eds.), *Perspectives on the World Christian Movement: A Reader* (Pasadena: William Carey, 1981).

4. G.E. Ladd, "The Gospel of the Kingdom" in Winter R., *et al.* (eds.), *Perspectives on the World Christian Movement: A Reader* (Pasadena: William Carey, 1981), pp. 51-69.

5. See for example Pius Wakatama and James Shearer cited in the bibliography.

6. See David Bosch, *Transforming Mission* (New York, Orbis Books, 1991), p. 11.

7. See Sir Fred Catherwood, *A Better Way* (London, IVP).

8. See Peter Atkins, *Good News in Evangelism* (Auckland: St John, 1991).

9. See Cyril Okorocha, "The Meaning of Salvation" in William Dyrness, *Two Thirds World Theologies* (Zondervan, 1993).

10. See Cyril Okorocha, "The Meaning of Religious Conversion in Africa: its missiological impliations" (Geneva, Mission Studies, 1992) and *The Meaning of Religious Conversion in Africa* (Aldershot, U.K.: Avebury, 1987)

for a discussion of the missiological advantages of such an holistic understanding of the *Missio Dei*.

11. See further Cyril Okorocha, "The Meaning of Religious Conversion in
Africa: its missiological implications" (Geneva, Mission Studies, 1992).

12. John Stott.

## Selected Bibliography

Atkins, Peter, *Good News in Evangelism* (Auckland: St. John, 1991).

Bediako, Kwame, *Theology and Identity* (Oxford: Regnum Books, 1992).

Bosch, David, *Transforming Mission* (New York: Orbis Books, 1991).

Carey, George, et. al., *A Transforming Vision. Report of the ACC/Primates
meeting Cape Town, January 1993* (London: Church House, 1993).

Craston, Colin, "An introduction and a plea" in Craston, (ed.), *By Word and
Deed* (London: Church House, 1992), pp. xi-xxi.

Forster, Richard, *Money Sex and Power* (London: Hodder, 1991).

Fung, Raymond, *Yours Evangelistically* (Geneva: WCC, 1992).

John-Paul II, *Redemptoris Missio. Encyclical on Missionary Activity*, Origins,
20 (34), 1991.

Ladd, G E, "The Gospel on the Kingdom" in Winter, *et al.* (eds.), *Perspectives
on the World Christian Movement* (Pasadena: William Carey, 1981), pp.
51-69.

Luther-King, Jr. Martin, *Strength to Love, Trumpet of Conscience*.

Mowday, Lois, *The Snare* (Southampton: Navpress, 1988).

Okorocha Cyril C., *The Meaning of Religious Conversion in Africa* (Aldershot,
UK: Avebury, 1987).

————, "The Meaning of Religious Conversion in Africa: its missiological implications" (Geneva: Mission Studies, 1992).

————, "The Church Exists for Mission" in *EFAC Bulletin* (1992).

————, "What is the Spirit saying" in *Anglican World/Compasrose*, June
'93 (London: ACC).

————, "The meaning of salvation," in Dyrness, Bill, ed., *Two Thirds
World Theologies* (Zondervan, 1993).

Pobee, John S., *AD 2000 and Beyond* (Ghana: Asempa, 1991).

————, *Skenosis* (Ghana: Asempa, 1991).

Shearer, James, *Missionary go Home* (New Jersey: Prentice Hall, 1964).

Stott, John R.W., "The Bible in World Evangelization" in Winter R., *et al.*
(eds.), *Perspectives on the World Christian Movement: A Reader* (Pasadena:
William Carey, 1981).

————, *The Message of Acts* (London: IVP, 1991).

Theresa, Revd. Mother, *Love until it hurts*.

Tutu, Desmond, *Hope and Suffering in South Africa*.

Wakatama, Pius, *Independence for the Third World Church* (Downer's Grove:
IVP, 1976).

# Scripture in Ecumenical Dialogue

*Michael Nazir Ali*

### The Authority of Scripture in Scripture

I wish to begin with the authority of scripture as it is recognized in scripture itself. Within the Old Testament there is considerable veneration of the Torah, the bedrock of God's revelation of himself. In the so called Deuteronomistic history, for example, there are many references to the law of Moses already, and, of course, the second Book of Kings recounts the discovery of the Book of the Law and how the nation of Israel and its king responded to this.[1]

By the time of writing of the Apocryphal Books the three-fold division of the Hebrew scriptures is well established, that is to say, the Law, the Prophets and the Sacred Writings. Both Jesus, and a little later Josephus, referred to this three-fold division.[2]

Jesus is continually quoting from the Hebrew scriptures, in respect of his own person and ministry, for instance. He speaks of himself as the divine Son of Man who is to come in glory at the close of the age, referring back, of course, to the great images in the Book of Daniel (e.g., Mk. 13:24-28 and parallels of Dan. 7:13-14). Jesus speaks of himself in terms of the Messianic Psalms (see Ps. 72, Mk. 12:36 and Ps. 110:1). He speaks of himself in terms of the Suffering Servant of the second part of the Book of Isaiah (Mk. 8:31-33, 10:45, etc.). He quotes from the Scriptures in his response to testing by the Devil all quotations are from the Book of Deuteronomy. He repeats "It is written" (Matt. 4:1-11 and parallels). He quotes from Scripture in justification of his works of mercy and against a rigid understanding of the law (Matt. 12.7).

Jesus quotes from Scripture in his teaching on purity, forgiveness, the inner life and trust in God. Look, for example, at the allusions to the Old Testament in the Beatitudes and in his appeal to the priority of one principle in Scripture over another. For instance, in appealing to the creation ordinance of marriage over and against the Mosaic law of divorce. (When I was a parish priest in Pakistan I found that Muslim women attending Christian weddings never failed to be impressed if we read Mark 10 as the Gospel for that occasion.) So Jesus appeals to the creation ordinance of marriage over and against the Mosaic law of divorce. He also quotes Scripture in arguing for the priority of works of mercy against a rigid adherence to cultic requirements and the rubric here is taken from Hosea 6:6: "I desire mercy and not sacrifice."

## Scripture in the Early Church

In its proclamation of the crucified, risen and ascended Christ the early Church repeatedly referred to the prophecies about the Messiah in the Old Testament and appealed to Scripture for support over a number of other issues; obvious examples are the kerygmatic speeches in the Book of the Acts of the Apostles. In the New Testament, even where there is a critical engagement with the Hebrew scriptures with regard to the place of the law, for instance, there is always a tacit acknowledgement, at least, of the primacy of Scripture. Take St. Paul's argument in the Epistle to the Romans. Paul contrasts life in the Spirit with the law which brings awareness only of sin and death, and yet he is moved to say the law is holy and the commandment is holy, just and good (Rom. 7:12).

In the early Church there was great emphasis on the rule of faith, basic belief for all Christians. But this rule of faith is derived from scriptural testimony and, as Geoffrey Lampe used to say, the rule of faith in turn enables the Church to recognize what is authentically Scripture for there is a mutuality here. The Fathers have numerous references to the authority and primacy of the

Scriptures but I want to refer just to two, one from the East and one from the 'West' – by the 'West' I mean North Africa, of course! The first reference is to Origen. Origen is perhaps the father of speculative theology. But in his commentary on the First Epistle to the Corinthians he refers to Paul's injunction not to go beyond what is written and defends the priority of Scripture, particularly in relation to those who claimed an independent esoteric tradition handed down by the Apostles. So already in Origen we have a view against a two-source theory of revelation. Origen is not denying the possibility or value of speculative theology. Even a superficial reading of his work would show us that, but what he is saying is that such a theology needs to be based on Scripture. We may disagree with Origen's view of Scripture and how he used it, but he certainly recognized its primacy.

## Augustine

St. Augustine is quoted often in ecumenical dialogue. Augustine is quite clear that the Church herself recognizes and confirms the intrinsic authority of the Scriptures; that the apostles, the bishops, the synods of the Church have served only to recognize and to confirm this intrinsic authority of Scripture and that no other authority can be compared with it. The authority of Scripture, he says, is above the authority of any person however catholic and this has to be set against his oft-quoted sentence, "I would not have believed the Gospel, if it had not been for the authority of the Catholic Church." Even Roman Catholic theologians now say that this does not mean that Augustine is setting the Church above the Bible but only that it is in the Church that the universality of the Gospel is displayed and its authority acknowledged.[3]

## The Middle Ages and the Reformation

As the Middle Ages went on, this clear recognition of the primacy of scripture began to change and there are several reasons for this change. The dominance of superstition is certainly one of them; as more and more of the world became Christianized there was bad as well as good inculturation and contextualization. There were many superstitions that came into the Church and obscured the clarity of this belief. The emergence and the development of very exaggerated claims to ecclesiastical authority also obscured the primary authority of Scripture. And thirdly, this is perhaps more controversial, the re-discovery of Aristotle also affected the use of Scripture in theological method.

But at the same time movements of reform, as they emerged in the later Middle Ages, although very different from each other, all seemed to have in common that they recognized the primacy of the authority of Scripture. So it is not something that began with the Reformation, but was present already in seed in earlier times; during the 'first Reformation' as it were. At the Reformation itself, this was one of the great issues between those who wanted to continue the medieval tradition in the Church and those who wanted renewal and reform.

What is the place of Scripture in the life of the Church? The Anglican tradition, as one of the reformed traditions, also developed a particular approach to scripture. This was vis-a-vis the view that was emerging already at the Council of Trent; against the 'partly-partly' two-source approach, but it was also developed in relation to certain aspects of the Continental Reformation where there were some who were making Scripture prescriptive for the minutest details of life. Paul Avis claims that the Anglican tradition in its view of Scripture, can be spoken of as a consensus from Hooker to the Anglican Newman.[4] In spite of differences in approach, method and emphases, there is a consensus among Anglican theologians of many different kinds on this central matter that was at issue at that time and still is today. This has provided Anglicanism with a certain theological coherence.

## The Anglican Consensus

There are five aspects to this Anglican consensus as it has existed in history. First, that the Scriptures are sufficient for salvation. This is found even today in almost every Anglican ordinal. Secondly, that in this respect they are utterly reliable. Thirdly, that in the matter of saving truth they are entirely perspicuous even to the simple. Fourth, that the Scriptures are not prescriptive for every area of individual or church life but that there is a certain amount of evangelical liberty in ordering

our personal and corporate lives in the light of scriptural principle. In particular, the Church at different levels has a responsibility for its own ceremonial and government in fidelity to the
Scriptures. There is also the question of *adiaphora*, the things
indifferent; whether Christians should go to the theatre or to the
bar after the evening session, was left to the people's conscience
I am glad to say! Then, fifthly, authoritative teachers, such as
bishops, are competent to interpret scripture and tradition where
they are not clear or where they need to be related to contemporary circumstances, but this does not make such teachers infallible in themselves. If their teaching is to be received by the faithful
it should manifestly be consonant with Scripture and with apostolic tradition. So the doctrine of reception emerges in Anglican
thinking at a fairly early stage.

There is, therefore, an Anglican view of Scripture. But at the
same time all the churches of the Reformation agreed, and still
agree, on the primacy of Scripture, and agreement on the primacy of Scripture is what has made cooperation possible in
mission between the churches of the Reformation. For example,
in the translation, production and dissemination of the Scriptures themselves; the work of the Bible Society, almost the first
example of interdenominational cooperation in mission, became
possible because there was this agreement.[5]

## The Orthodox Churches

The Orthodox and the Roman Catholic Churches have joined
this movement comparatively late. Of course, the Anglican tradition was in ecumenical dialogue with other churches from the
very earliest times. The polemical dialogues with the Roman
Catholics are only one example of this. There was also friendly
contact. James II, just prior to his exile, laments the disappearance
of friendship between Roman Catholics and Anglicans.[6] But
there was also continuing friendly relationship and interchange
with the Continental churches of the Reformation. There had
been ecumenical contact with the great Eastern and Oriental
Churches since the Reformation, but the first serious negotiations with the Eastern Churches came about with the movement
of the Non-jurors.

## The Non-jurors

The Non-jurors were those bishops, clergy and laity who, in all conscience, could not take the Oath of Allegiance to William and Mary having first taken an oath to the exiled James. The Archbishop of Canterbury of the time was among them, and so they formed an *ecclesiola*, as it were, in this country for over a hundred years and because they were a smallish group, they wanted wider fellowship. Despite accusations that they were crypto-Catholics, they did not look to Rome for such fellowship, but to the Eastern Churches. Now most of the Non-jurors came, actually, from what we would call a high church tradition, and so they were very open to some kind of rapprochement with the Orthodox. The negotiations went on for a long time. They addressed several 'humble supplications' to the Orthodox Patriarchs and received in reply some very haughty letters, but they took the haughtiness of these letters and continued with the negotiations.

In the end the negotiations broke down on five issues and I just wish to recount them because they may have some contemporary significance. First, the Non-Jurors, mostly high church Anglicans, could not put the authority of tradition on the same level as the authority of Scripture as the Patriarchs demanded they should. Secondly, the Non-Jurors honoured Mary the Blessed *Theotokos* but were afraid of the Marian cult in Orthodoxy as much as in Rome. Thirdly, they had scruples about the invocation of the saints. Fourth, although they worshipped Christ as truly present in the Eucharist they could not subscribe to the cult of adoring the symbols of that presence. Fifthly, they could not agree to the worship of icons as required as a matter of faith by the Patriarchs. In addition to these five difficulties that they experienced, we might also add the doctrine of justification by faith alone.

This was the grand question, as Hooker put it, that hung between Rome and Anglicans, and not only between Rome and Anglicans, but between Anglicans and the Orthodox. In fact, both Eastern and Oriental Orthodox Churches have recent history of disciplining people within those Churches who have come to believe in this great doctrine. You will have seen in the

Church press recently certain evangelical, charismatic Anglican leaders asking charismatic Anglicans to join Orthodoxy. All I would want to say at this stage is, "well, maybe this is a way for some, but before people go that way they should consider the difficulties of the Non-Jurors!"[7]

## The Anglican Principle

Now coming to more recent dialogue and its basis. I think we must trace modern Anglican interest in ecumenism to F.D. Maurice and to William Reed Huntington. Willing Reed Huntington was an American Episcopalian theologian who began to distinguish between what he called the *Anglican system* and what he called the *Anglican principle*. The system for him was spires, choristers, Trollopian archdeacons and evensong in Canterbury Cathedral; all these wonderful things! He saw that these things had value in certain contexts but not in all contexts and particularly, he felt, not in North America in the 19th century. The Anglican principle, on the other hand, which the system sometimes obscured, was what was really valuable about Anglicanism and something that Anglicanism could bring to the world Church.

There are two poles to the Anglican principle as far as Huntington was concerned. One is the pole of locality, and for him this pole has to do with the local church's vocation to be and to become the catholic church in that place. This is not an invention of Huntington's. It is already referred to in the Articles of Religion and in the Preface to the Book of Common Prayer, the calling of the local church, to be and to become the catholic church in a particular place. But the other pole is the pole of catholicity. How are these local churches authentically 'church' in their own place, in fellowship with other local churches also authentically church in their own place? Huntington identified four bases for this fellowship. First, the authority of the Scriptures; secondly, an acknowledgement of the authority of the historic creeds, the Apostles and Nicene Creeds; thirdly, the acknowledgement of the dominical sacraments of Baptism and the Eucharist, and finally the historic three-fold ministry of the Church. These, for Huntington, not only constituted the basis of fellowship among Anglicans but constituted also a charter for discussion on unity with other churches and, of course, this later aspect of Huntington's work became better known. In 1886 the Chicago General Convention of the Episcopal Church in the USA accepted these points of William Reed Huntington's as a basis for dialogue with other Churches in the United States of America. In 1888 the Lambeth Conference accepted what is now known as the *Chicago-Lambeth Quadrilateral* as a basis for approach for Christian unity.[8]

## The Lambeth Quadrilateral

The Lambeth Quadrilateral has been accused by some Catholic Anglicans of being minimalist, as it is. It is deliberately minimalist because it seeks unity and not uniformity. For example, it promotes the historic three-fold ministry of the Church as a way of ordering the Church but not any particular interpretation or theological understanding of it. It is minimalist because it promotes respect for liberty of conscience and sets minimum parameters for unity. It seeks to bring diversity and even, perhaps, disagreement into a unity which is based on primitive Christian faith and order. The Lambeth Quadrilateral, as enunciated by the 1888 Lambeth Conference, refers to the Holy Scriptures as containing all things necessary to salvation and of being the rule and ultimate standard of faith, so that has been a basis of an Anglican approach to ecumenical discussion as far as Scripture is concerned. Lambeth 1920's appeal to all Christian people for unity resulted in a plethora of ecumenical conversations, including conversations about the union of churches in Asia, in the subcontinent of what is now India and Pakistan, and it is interesting that the first report about union in South India came to the 1930 Lambeth Conference. The plans for Church Union at regional and national level, particularly in India, strengthened the Quadrilateral's first point by referring to the Scriptures not simply as the rule and ultimate standard of faith, but as the supreme and decisive standard of faith and in this strengthened way the plans of union were accepted by the different uniting churches.[9]

## The Roman Catholic Church

The entry of the Roman Catholic Church into the world of ecumenical dialogue has changed, I believe, the emphasis of ecumenical dialogue from a regional or national level to international bi-lateral and multi-lateral dialogue. This is an interesting and little noticed fact about ecumenism in recent years and may have something to do with the structures of the Roman Catholic Church itself. In these international bi-lateral and multi-lateral dialogues, in which Anglicans are involved, of course, Scripture seems to be used in three main ways.

First, the dialogues refer to those portions of Scripture which exhort Christians to unity – St. John chapter 17, the high priestly prayer of Jesus, is obviously a key text here, but 1 Corinthians 12, Ephesians 1 and 4 and other texts are also important. Secondly, they appeal to Scripture to establish certain doctrines. The ARCIC statement on the Eucharist, for instance, makes extended use of the term *anamnesis* as it is used in the Scriptures and the Fathers to describe how in the Eucharist the once for all sacrifice of Christ becomes effective in the present through the action of the Holy Spirit. Another example is the way in which the so-called Petrine texts are used in the second statement on Authority by ARCIC to establish Peter's primacy in the apostolic band, for example, the fact that Peter's name occurs first in every list.

Second, some theologians, such as Alister McGrath, feel that ARCIC's handling of Scripture in certain areas, has been somewhat superficial when compared with the detailed exegesis and documentation of say, the Lutheran-Roman Catholic dialogue; McGrath's point, which is also made by some others, is that the ARCIC method of enunciating the results of historical and exegetical work without documenting these results is something that gives rather a bland 'take it or leave it' air to the ARCIC documents. This is not present in, say, the Lutheran-Roman Catholic dialogue where there is painstaking exegesis of the Biblical texts and where the history and the theology of a particular matter is taken seriously along with the convergences and continuing divergences as well as a reconstruction of doctrine that may be acceptable to both churches. An example of this is the Lutheran-Roman Catholic document *Justification by Faith*. McGrath points out that this runs to 24,000 words and 218 quite substantial footnotes, as well as an accompanying book edited by John Reumman called *Righteousness in the New Testament* with scholars both Roman Catholic and Lutheran contributing to it. By contrast, 'Salvation and the Church', the Anglican-Roman Catholic document, runs to 6,000 words and has 5 footnotes including an obscure one about Hooker.[10]

Third, these dialogues discuss the place of Scripture in the Church's life. The different dialogues refer to the authority of Scripture in various ways. First of all, they refer to Scripture as "a normative record of the authentic foundation of faith" (AR-CIC). The Meissen agreement refers to scripture as "the authentic record of God's revelation in Jesus Christ" and "as the norm for Christian faith and life." By contrast the Niagara Report, another Anglican-Lutheran document, merely declares that "we accept the authority of the canonical scriptures of the Old and New Testaments." The Anglican-Reformed dialogue *God's Reign and our Unity* speaks of the Scriptures as "the authoritative standard of faith" and then, finally, the Anglican-Orthodox dialogue says that the Scriptures "bear authoritative witness to God's revelation of himself in creation, in the incarnation of the Word and in the whole history of salvation."[11]

## Problems in Recent Ecumenical Dialogue

Some problems have arisen nevertheless in recent ecumenical dialogue in relation to Scripture; first, the problem of how Scripture relates to tradition, authority and development in the faith and life of the Church. This is discussed most fully in the Anglican-Roman Catholic and the Anglican-Orthodox dialogues. It is very encouraging that both dialogues speak of Scripture in very high terms, so the Orthodox dialogue, while rejecting the two source theory of revelation, affirms that Scripture is the main criterion whereby the Church tests traditions to determine whether they are authentically Christian or not. Similarly, the elucidations for the ARCIC first Report on Authority speak of the Scriptures as the primary norm for Christian faith and life. Authority II, in discussing the role of the Roman Pontiff in the discernment of truth, acknowledges that Anglicans could accept such a ministry only if such a ministry were to be exercised in fidelity to biblical faith and orthodox tradition. At the same time, we need to note that what is agreed in the course of ecumenical dialogue, where the two sides have got to know each other well, may not be acceptable to the sponsoring churches. This is seen clearly in the Vatican's response to the ARCIC Final Report. The response rejects the ARCIC notion that the exercise of Papal or conciliar authority would only be acceptable if it is received by the faithful as manifestly a legitimate interpretation of the Gospel. For the Vatican, and I quote from the response, "the certain knowledge of any defined truth is not guaranteed by the reception of the faithful that such is in conformity with scripture and tradition, but by the authoritative definition itself on the part of the authentic teachers."[12]

In other words, such teaching is of its very nature consonant with the Scriptures and does not need to be demonstrated to be so consonant! This is a kind of ecclesiastical fundamentalism and goes right back to the claim that it is the Church that is the single interpreter of the Scriptures and by the Church, of course, is meant the *Magisterium*. Also, this ecclesiastical fundamentalism results in a curious view of the Scriptures.

The response to ARCIC I's mild questioning as to whether, as a result of historical and critical study, the Petrine texts could be taken to establish the immediate and direct institution of the Papacy by Jesus himself is rejected by the Vatican and an appeal is made once again to the living tradition of the Church. And so we are back to the two sources of Trent despite the labours of so many in the ecumenical dialogue![13] The Orthodox dialogues seem more open to the possibility of reception by the faithful of official teaching.

In both dialogues, however, there lurks the question of the custodianship of Scripture. Are the clergy the sole custodians of Scripture and do the rest of the faithful simply receive what they teach or do the laity have a more important and more pro-active role in the understanding of Scripture and in its application to contemporary life? The Anglican, as well as other reformers, certainly regarded the teaching of the Scriptures as plain to everyone, at least as far as matters of salvation are concerned. The availability of the Bible to the laity was a particular feature of the Reformation and today the role of the laity in the formulation of the Church's mind on issues of faith and order is preserved in the structures of synodical government. This is an important difference. Even the word 'synod' has different meanings in the Roman Catholic Church and in the Anglican tradition.

In ecumenical dialogue Anglicans need to remain faithful, then, to the consensus from Hooker to the Anglican Newman on the sufficiency on the Scriptures for salvation, their reliability and their perspicuity in this respect and their general availability to the faithful. Teachers in the Church still have a significant role to play in bringing out all the treasures of the Scriptures for the Church as a whole and in recalling and re-emphasizing important truths. They are also important in leading the whole Church to discern which developments in its faith and life are according to Scripture and bring out the implications of scripture, its mind, its *phronema*.

### Inculturation and Contextualization

It is here that the teachers are important in the twin tasks of inculturation and contextualization. Inculturation I take to mean making the Gospel at home and making the Church at home in a particular culture with reference to its traditions, its world view and its values. Contextualization I take to mean making the Gospel at home in particular social, economic and political circumstances. Bishop David Gitari, at the Lambeth Conference, in this very university in 1988, made some distinction about what the Gospel affirms in particular cultures, what it may tolerate for the time being and what the Gospel must reject.[14] Pope John Paul II, also, in a very important Encyclical on Mission, has pointed out that there must be a limit set to the processes of inculturation and of contextualization. For him these limits are two. There is first of all the limit set by the gospel itself, nothing can be done that is contrary to the gospel and, secondly, there is the limit which is set by the necessity of continuing fellowship between local churches.[15] Christopher Duraisingh of the World Council of Churches speaks of *criteria* for contextualization and inculturation rather than limits, but here too, there is a concern about the necessity of testing the authenticity of inculturation and contextualization. Inculturation and contextualization also need to be related to reflection on how to evaluate developments in the secular world in the light of Scripture.

In discussions on unity, we should be clear that in any united church the Scriptures will be acknowledged as the supreme and decisive standard of faith, a standard, moreover, to which both teachers and the rest of the faithful must submit. In such a church the Scriptures must be freely available and used not only in corporate liturgical worship, but for private study and devotion, as well as in small groups. The rigorous study of the Scriptures will be encouraged and church pronouncements on doctrine and practice will be made only when such study in its textual, literary and historical forms has been firmly taken into account. Such provisions will prevent a united church from being either fundamentalist or authoritarian. At the same time, it will be a church firmly grounded in the historic faith, with reverence for the sources of faith and obedience to the rule of faith.

## Notes

1. See further the introduction to A.D.H. Mayes, *Deuteronomy*, NCBC, (Grand Rapids: Eerdmans, 1947), pp. 41f.

2. R.K. Harrison, *Introduction to the Old Testament* (London: IVP, 1970), pp. 260ff.

3. Origen, *Commentary on 1 Corinthians* and Augustine, *Against Faustus* and *Letter to Fortunatianus* in R.B. Eno, SS, *Teaching Authority in the Early Church* (Delaware: Michael Glazier, 1984).

4. P. Avis, *Anglicanism and the Christian Church* (Edinburgh: T & T Clark, 1989), p. 66.

5. D.W. Bebbington, *Evangelicals in Modern Britain* (London: Unwin, 1989), p. 66.

6. J. Miller, *James II: A Study in Kingship* (Hove, 1978).

7. J.H. Overton, *The Non-Jurors* (London: Smith Elder, 1902), pp. 451ff.

8. See further Reed Huntington, *The Church Idea. An Essay Towrds Unity*, 4th edn. (New York, 1899), and J.R. Wright (ed.), *Quadrilateral at One Hundred* (Cincinnati: Forward Movement, 1988).

9. W.J. Marshall, *Faith and Order in the North India/Pakistan Unity Plan: A Theological Assessment* (London, 1978), pp. 14f.

10. See A. McGrath, *ARCIC II and Justification: An Evangelical-Anglican Assessment of 'Salvation and the Church'* (Oxford: Latimer House, 1987). Also, *Justification by Faith: Lutheran-Roman Catholic Dialogue Group in the USA*, Origins, NC Documentary Service, Washington DC, 6 October 1983; *Salvation and the Church: ARCIC II* (London: CTS/CHP, 1987).

11. ARCIC, *The Final Report* (London: CTS/SPCK, 1982), Authority in the Church I, Sec 2; *On the Way to Visible Unity: Meissen 1988* (London: BMU, 1988), Sec. 9; *The Niagara Report* (London: CHP, 1988), Sec. 61; *God's Reign*

*and Our Unity* (London and Edinburgh: SPCK/ St Andrews, 1984), Sec. 40; *Anglican-Orthodox Dialogue: The Dublin Argued Statement* (London: SPCK, 1984), Appendix I, II:4.

12. *Response of the Holy See to the Final Report of the ARCIC* (London: CTS, 1991), p. 8.

13. Ibid., pp. 11f.

14. The address is published in V. Samuel and A. Hauser (eds.), *Proclaiming Christ in Christ's Way: Studies in Integral Evangelism* (Oxford: Regnum Books, 1989), Ch. 7, pp. 101ff.

15. "Redemptionis Missio: Evangelical Letter on the Permanent Validity of the Church's Missionary Mandate" in *Catholic International*, Paris, 15-31 March, 1991.

# Scripture in Ecumenical Dialogue
## A Response to Bishop Michael Nazir Ali

*Margaret Rodgers*

We would all agree that the WCC is not the ultimate reposi-
tory of the ecumenical tradition, nor the source of all ecumenical
endeavours, though it holds the prominent place in the ecumenical arena. Its new General Secretary, Konrad Raiser, wrote:

> ... the WCC has repeatedly described itself as "an instrument
> of the ecumenical movement," even as its "privileged instru-
> ment." This claim has also been expressly confirmed in the
> conversations with the Roman Catholic Church. The ecu-
> menical movement is not identical with the WCC, but extends
> beyond the actually existing churches. "Instrument of the
> ecumenical movement" — does that mean agent for renewal
> and change as opposed to interest in preservation, continuity
> and maintaining the *status quo*? The ecumenical organizations
> are nothing without the churches, but at the same time their
> *raison d'etre* lies in calling the churches out of the parochialism
> of their confessional or national existence.[1]

Because of the dimension of that claim I am focussing my
response to Bishop Michael's paper towards the WCC which
itself engages in multi-lateral dialogue and discussions. For
many people it provides the ecumenical context.

Of course, the multi-lateral and bi-lateral conversations are
on the whole the stuff of a rarefied world inhabited by a small

number of specialists. I recall what happened when people from the small inner city congregation I belong to in Sydney joined with people from the local Catholic parish to discuss *Salvation and the Church*. A good deal of work had been done by a group appointed by the two Archbishops to prepare studies on this ARCIC text. When our people from St. Stephen's met with the people from St. Joseph's the discussions were about everything else but the said text. People told each other their faith stories, they were so excited to be together. For they saw the value in their meeting and said they did not want to talk about *Salvation and the Church*. It belonged to the theologians, not to them. If we are addressing the issues of ecumenical dialogue we need to take this into account. I fear our multi-lateral and bi-lateral conversations would appear to be of only peripheral interest to most people in the pews!

## Concessions

Günther Gassmann of the WCC staff visited Australia in 1992. In the course of one of his addresses (which focussed on Scripture and Tradition) he said this:

> The ecumenical movement began with one basic assumption and encouragement: despite all the bitter divisions which scandalously divide us we are not only drawn together by the love of God in Jesus Christ, which we all experience and confess, but also by a common basis which we all share: this basis is the Holy Scripture which for all of us constitute the supreme authority of faith and life. And one should add that, with all the modifications and differentiations which this initial assumption has received in the course of eighty years of ecumenical theological dialogue, it remains valid and effective until today. In fact, it would seem that it should even receive more attention and serious reflection today than is often the case because otherwise we will leave one indispensable and essential source of Christian communion to our evangelical colleagues and thereby cut ourselves off from any possibility of involving the evangelical movement in the broader stream of the one ecumenical movement.[2]

There are a number of underlying concessions in that statement — for instance that there has been an ecumenical journey regarding the concept of the authority of Scripture; that the doctrine appears to be receiving less acknowledgement and focus in contemporary ecumenical circles; that focus on the authority of Scripture is being left unassailed to evangelicals who are accordingly indifferent to or critical of the conciliar ecumenical movement for its neglect or misuse of Scripture. The statement appears to argue that one reason for the WCC circles giving attention to the authority of Scripture is to keep the evangelicals in or to involve them, which is scarcely a worthy motive, even if that is what Günther did mean to say.

### Statements

There have been a number of useful publications which discuss the place and use of Scripture in the WCC. The following statements are generally accepted.

a. The authority of the Bible was the unquestioned and essential presupposition of the early ecumenical movement. At the New Delhi Assembly (1961) Visser't Hooft, then the General Secretary stated "the Bible is the voice that gives the WCC its marching orders."

b. Though this is the case, even as early as the Lausanne Faith and Order Conference in 1927, the theme of the relationship between scripture and tradition drew some attention. In response to one report "The Church's Message to the World — the Gospel" the view was accepted that it was God's saving initiative in Jesus Christ through the Holy Spirit which provided the deepest bond of unity and not simply the formal recognition of the canon or of the authority of Holy Scripture. Gassmann commented that this acceptance has become a fundamental inspiration of the ecumenical movement of lasting significance.

c. At the Edinburgh Faith and Order Conference in 1937 the relationship of Scripture, Tradition and the Church was discussed, and the differing positions became clear. The report says:

> We are one in recognizing that the Church, enlightened by the Holy Spirit, has been instrumental in the formation of the Bible. But some of us hold that this implies that the Church under the guidance of the Spirit is entrusted with the author-

ity to explain, interpret and complete (*symleroun*) the teaching of the Bible, and consider the witness of the Church as given in tradition as equally authoritative with the Bible itself. Others, however, believe that the Church, having recognized the Bible as the indispensable record of the revealed Word of God, is bound exclusively by the Bible as the only rule of faith and practice and, while accepting the relative authority of tradition, would consider it authoritative only in so far as it is founded upon the Bible itself.[3]

On the one side Scripture and the Church teaching authoritatively held together, on the other side Scripture as the sole rule and standard of faith.

d. The theological base of the WCC in its constitution did not refer to Scripture as a common ground, but to the Christological centre of the Christian faith — probably through the influence of the "Biblical theology" school. The words "according to the Scriptures" was added in 1961 at New Delhi, a change first requested by the Lutheran Church of Norway in 1953. The recent WCC Moderator, Bishop Held, wrote in 1985 that this addition to the Basis ". . . was not in fact something new, but rather the expression of a universal Christian conviction."[4]

e. The Montreal Faith and Order Conference in 1963 may be seen as a watershed in WCC attitudes to the Scripture. At that conference Roman Catholic theologians participated actively and the Orthodox participation was more representative and intensive than in earlier gatherings. So the two major protagonists of the place of tradition were well to the fore. Therefore this conference emphasized strongly the place of tradition in the church, noting the interlinkage of tradition and Scripture. Side by side, it was said, they were authoritative — there is *Tradition* (that is, "the Gospel itself transmitted through the generations in and by the Church"), and there is *traditions* (that is, the diversity of forms of expression and also confessional traditions). At this conference Ernst Käsemann presented a very influential address. Through the impact of that address the underlying sense of a diversity of theologies *within* the Bible entered ecumenical discussion.

f. As a consequence another question from Montreal was "Do

all the traditions which claim to be Christian contain the Tradition? By what criterion are they evaluated?" The answer — the major criterion is the appeal to Scripture 'rightly interpreted' — but what is 'right interpretation'? The report refers to a range of different hermeneutical principles used in various traditions.

> In some confessional traditions the accepted hermeneutical principle has been that any portion of Scripture is to be interpreted in the light of Scripture as a whole. In others the key has been sought in what is considered to be the centre of Holy Scripture, and the emphasis has been primarily on the Incarnation, or on the Atonement and Redemption, or on justification by faith, or again on the message of the nearness of the Kingdom of God, or on the ethical teachings of Jesus. In yet others, all emphasis is laid upon what Scripture says to the individual conscience, under the guidance to the Holy Spirit. In the Orthodox Church the hermeneutical key is found in the mind of the Church, especially as expressed in the Fathers of the Church and in the Ecumenical Councils. In the Roman Catholic Church the hermeneutical key is found in the deposit of faith, of which the Church's *magisterium* is the guardian. In other traditions again the creeds, complemented by confessional documents or by the definitions of Ecumenical Councils and the witness of the Fathers, are considered to give the right key to the understanding of Scripture. In none of these cases where the principle of interpretation is found elsewhere than in Scripture is the authority thought to be alien to the central concept of Holy Scripture. On the contrary, it is considered as providing just a key to the understanding of what is said in Scripture.[5]

g. Faith and Order meetings in Bristol (1967) and Louvain (1971) pursued the question of right interpretation given that range of hermeneutical possibilities. Though Bristol held that "the Bible is a given fact in the Church" it accepted that there are diversities within the Scripture itself. At Louvain James Barr was an influential voice. He raised the question of whether there was basic theological disagreement internal to the Scripture, which would demand a choice of preference of Scripture against Scripture. This would have the consequence of raising a fundamental doubt as to the validity of the Scriptural truth, even if 'rightly interpreted'.

h. In its report Louvain answered the question "How are we to approach the Bible so that, through the Biblical text, God may speak to us authoritatively today?" This question infers that something more is needed than the fact that God caused the Scripture to be written before it is to be regarded as authoritative. Louvain said our experience must attest to its authority. This added to the ecumenical agenda an "hermeneutic of experience" — a subjective, relativizing hermeneutic. Under the influence of Barr and Ellen Flesseman-van Leer, Louvain said "[Biblical] authority is therefore a present reality only when men (sic) experience it as authority; at the same time it transcends human experience." Paul Schrotenboer's comment on this is:

> Little wonder that following this extensive discussion the great stress of the WCC has fallen far more on the situation or context of the Bible than on the Bible itself. For it is in the current context that our experience occurs. It should therefore be no surprise that [here he mentions name of the then General Secretary] should state that to appeal to what the Bible says has become out of date.[6]

This development of thought led to the much discussed question in the Preface to the 1982 Lima document *Baptism, Eucharist and Ministry* (BEM) that is, *"the extent to which your Church can recognize in the text the faith of the ages?"* The 180 responses received from churches indicated a non-reception of the "Montreal and post-Montreal clarifications on Scripture and Tradition." In his Australian address Günther Gassmann indicated that the staff in Geneva were surprised, but who would share their surprise if they moved from the perspective of member Churches true to their theological or confessional traditions? The 1990 Faith and Order report on the BEM responses indicated six different ways of viewing the relationship between Scripture and Tradition which may be detected in the contributions from the churches. These are:

a. Scripture is the only authority for faith and life.

b. Scripture and the Tradition of the early church are authoritative.

c. Scripture, the ancient creeds and later confessions are authoritative.

d. Scripture, Tradition and a teaching office of the church are decisive.

e. Scripture, Tradition and reason are valid criteria.

f. The tradition of the gospel as witnessed in Scripture and transmitted through the ages is the basis.[7] (This is the Montreal perspective.)

Our discussions about Scripture in the ecumenical tradition must take all of the above into account. When representatives of the churches come together in ecumenical dialogue these are the perspectives upon the Scripture which they bring and which must be harmonized into some kind of ecumenical convergence in the reports they produce. Little wonder that so many go home feeling that their views are underrepresented or disregarded. For they represent both the theological movements of the day and also the confessional traditions, and not singly but in their diversity.

The hermeneutic of experience has been reinforced by various liberatory theologies enthusiastically endorsed in ecumenical circles. These first became prominent in the 1970s and today it may be said that these theologies with their contextualized hermeneutic appear to dominate much of the WCC agenda — though not nearly so much to this point in the Faith and Order stream of activity.

Scripture in its plain meaning is sometimes easily set aside. I have not forgotten the day when, in our Section plenary meeting, an African delegate attempted to have inserted into the text of our report words based on John 14:6. It related to a statement about encounter with other faiths. The sentence from the report reads "We witness to the truth that salvation is in Christ and we also remain open to other people's witness to truth as they have experienced it."[8] His amendment was rejected on two occasions, and so was one from a Scandinavian Lutheran who attempted to assist him. Words based on a relevant Scriptural text were excluded there on the pragmatic ground that to include them could hinder dialogue with other faiths — that was the argument presented against them and it won the day.

## Evangelical Anglican Assumptions

When I engage in ecumenical discussion, like everyone else, I take my own presuppositions and assumptions with me. I have been formed in an evangelical Anglican context which gives priority to the Scripture as the sole rule and standard and faith of life and which regards the Scripture specialist as the most essential contributor to theological discussion. Our theological and social/ethical work always commences with a careful review of the relevant Scriptural teaching and we move from the Scriptural perspective we thereby deduce into the issue which is our focus. We move from Scripture to context, and hopefully we bring a scripturally informed mind and conscience to the issue. There is a danger to this of course. It is that one can spend so much time on an investigation into the real meaning of the text in the context of the time in which it was written that the whole endeavour is focused on *that* question, and the process can descend into irrelevancy in regard to our own contemporary questions. I fear I know some whose careful Biblical analysis would appear to lead them into an unending journey into irrelevancy. Experts on the text, they are cut off from their own context. I am always grateful for the rich diversity of people and life situations which I meet in ecumenical circles and I benefit greatly, from the insight I am given into the reality of the life of many people in our world. I hear the cry for justice and my heart echoes it, but I still wish to move from Scripture to context. I do not regard this approach as an example of the imperialism of Western Scriptural method but rather as a mode of Scriptural inquiry appropriate to every culture which allows one to bring the word of the Gospel to bear upon culture and context — a priority of Scripture and Gospel over culture and context — including my own.

## Context to Text

The more prevalent hermeneutical method within WCC discussions gives priority to context and one moves from that into the Scripture. The danger of this approach is that the Scriptural work becomes irrelevant or else the Word is read only through the lens of the context. The meaning of the text in its original context becomes a word from the past, a mere historical irrelevancy. This hermeneutical approach has developed in recent years in that WCC stream of activity called Church and Society, which is the home of many we might feel tempted to call 'fundamentalist liberals'.

An informal group of church leaders and long-time friends of the WCC, a group which is chaired by the Archbishop of York, commented in mid-1992:

> The WCC at present has no coherent rationale for its method of using the Bible or for relating theological reflection to social ethics.[9]

For many people in the Church and Society stream of WCC activity their reading of Scripture allows Christ to become a metaphor for 'the suffering people' or 'the poor', whose context informs their interpretation, and their consequent reports. I offer you a quotation from an Asian theologian who is an active participant in Christian Conference of Asia as well as WCC activities. He is a proponent of the *Minjung* theology.

> How does one begin a Christological reflection on Jesus? I recommend a social biography of the *Minjung* as the locus of the Christological search. A story of the Korean Urban Industrial Mission (UIM) provides us with a starting point.

UIM workers began by reading the Bible with the workers, which led us to Jesus the worker, the son of a carpenter. Jesus was not a ruling elite, the *Yangban* in Korea; Jesus was simply *Minjung*. This was a remarkable and astonishing discovery on the part of the UIM workers, who graduated from seminary with a heavy dose of traditional Christology in their head. It was the workers who discovered Jesus the Worker. This became a "hermeneutical key" to the Biblical texts, opening a Christological upheaval.[10]

## JPIC

The comment from our Australian Anglican delegate to the 1990 Justice, Peace and the Integrity of Creation (JPIC) Convocation in Seoul focused in part on the theological framework of the JPIC draft document and the theological and Scriptural consensus which seemed to be operating. His comments were consonant with the views of many delegates after the WCC Assembly in Canberra. The JPIC vision appears to equate the Kingdom of God with particular political movements and struggles — in particular the poor, the people and the various social movements — and thus it 'idolizes' what are after all human, fallible and ambiguous political movements.

The focus of the vision shifts away from the person of Christ as the transcendent Lord to socio-political programmes for which 'Christ' becomes a metaphor providing ideological support. Christ is a metaphor for 'the poor' who are the bearers of salvation. Contra to that the teaching of the Scripture concerning the primary saving work of Christ in his death and resurrection should be used as a paradigm which gives meaning and hope to political struggles for justice. At Seoul the language of repentance and conversion was not oriented primarily to the person of Jesus — as the risen Lord — but to one's place within political struggles. This type of Scriptural and theological analysis has the effect of absolutizing political struggles as 'transcendent issues for our time'; it raises contemporary, radical, sociological analysis to a position of higher authority than Scripture since it fashions the hermeneutical key which interprets the Scripture; and it also has the effect of inhibiting a more dispassionate and less ideologically charged political analysis.

One wonders what will flow out of the International Faith and Order Conference which will be held in August 1993 in Spain if the JPIC emphasis is present 'to help build new models of ecclesiology which feature JPIC'[11] as one prominent Central Committee member argued recently? What influence will JPIC have on the Faith and Order outcomes? The WCC has recently published *Costly Unity: Koinonia and Justice Peace and the Integrity of Creation.* *Koinonia* is a New Testament term which has proved fruitful and seminal for ecumenical dialogue. However it now appears to be becoming somewhat of an ecumenical ragbag, the basis for every individual programme and idea. Will there be people there at the Faith and Order Conference in Spain to save *Koinonia* from collapsing under the weight it is being made to bear? If great care is not exercised in the use of *Koinonia* it may become a useless term as some are now suggesting about the word *unity*. Also the wide range of application given to *Koinonia* may result in people misreading and misunderstanding the term as it is used in the theology of the New Testament writers.

## Corrective

Can the evangelical with a high view of Scripture move comfortably in contemporary ecumenical circles, or in the world of ecumenical dialogue? It is easy to see why many forbear the politico-programmatic approach apparently dominant in so much WCC activity. But what the ecumenical agenda demands from us as evangelicals is that we cannot and must not ignore our contemporary context or the major questions of our time. We have much in common with those who act for justice in our world, for social action has always had its place in the evangelical agenda. But our commitment to Scriptural authority and to the right application of Scriptural truths are a grace and a gift and a necessary corrective which we should take with us into ecumenical relationships and discussions.

There are those who wait for such a voice and welcome it. For there are many friends from other theological and ecclesiological commitments who will receive with appreciation thoughtful evangelical contributions. We note one section of the reflections of the Orthodox participants at the Canberra Assembly.

> The tendency to marginalize the Basis in WCC work has created some dangerous trends in the WCC. We miss from many WCC documents the affirmation that Jesus Christ is the world's Saviour. We perceive a growing *departure from biblically-based Christian understandings* of: (a) the Trinitarian God; (b) salvation; (c) the "good news" of the gospel itself; (d) human beings as created in the image and likeness of God; and (e) the church, among others.[12]

Our evangelical statement at Canberra contained words somewhat consonant with those words, though perhaps not as sharply pointed.

> The ecumenical movement needs a theology rooted in the Christian revelation and [is] relevant to contemporary problems. At present, there is insufficient clarity regarding the relationship between the confession of the Lord Jesus Christ as God and Saviour according to scripture, the person and

work of the Holy Spirit, and legitimate concerns which are part of the WCC agenda.... This theological deficit not only conspires against the work of the WCC as a Christian witness but also increases the tensions among its member churches.[13]

Do we cut ourselves off from this ecumenical arena or do we keep ourselves in a position of involvement where we can influence and share with fellow Christians our view of the authority, integrity and sufficiency of Scripture? We must all make our own decision.

## Notes

1. Konrad Raiser, *Ecumenism in Transition: A Paradigm Shift in the Ecumenical Movement?* (Geneva: WCC, 1991), p. 26.

2. Günther Gassmann, *Scripture, Tradition and the Church: The Ecumenical Nexus in Faith and Order Work*, unpublished mss, Melbourne, 1992, pp. 1-2.

3. Gassmann, op. cit., p. 5.

4. Heinz-Joachim Held, "According to the Scriptures", *The Ecumenical Review*, Vol. 37, No. 2, 1985, p. 191.

5. Quoted in Paul G. Schrotenboer, "The Bible in the WCC," *Evangelical Review of Theology*, Vol. 2, No. 2, October 1978, p. 170.

6. Schrotenboer, op. cit., p. 175.

7. Gassmann, op. cit., p. 17.

8. Michael Kinnamon (ed.), *Signs of the Spirit: Official Report Seventh Assembly* (Geneva: WCC, 1991), p. 104.

9. "The Future of Ecumenical Social Thought," Report of an Informal Discussion of Church Leaders, Theologians, Social Ethicists, and Laity, Berlin, May 29 -June 3, 1992, mss copy, p. 5. This document was circulated to Heads of Churches and members of the Executive Committee of the Australian Council of Churches, by the General Secretary, the Revd David Gill who was a member of the informal group.

10. Kim Yong-Bock, *Messiah and Minjung: Christ's Solidarity with the People for New Life* (Hong Kong: CCA/URM, 1992), pp. 16-17.

11. Dr. Janice Love, "JPIC and the Future of the Ecumenical Movement," *The Ecumenical Review*, Vol. 42, No. 1, January 1991, p. 117.

12. Michael Kinnamon, op. cit., p. 280.

13. Michael Kinnamon, ibid., pp. 283-4. See also *Beyond Canberra* edited by Bruce Nicholls and Bong Rin Ro (Oxford: Regnum Books, 1994).

# Scripture and Social and Personal Morality

*Elaine Storkey*

## Introduction

It is often the case that in times of intense change people look back to something they call 'traditional morality'. Particularly in our secularized, modern, urban way of living in the West, social and personal morality have undergone a sea change. There are few ethical parameters which can now be taken for granted, few moral dictates which are not questioned or dismissed. In this climate the past can seem attractive with its patterns of greater stability, less mobility and higher degree of consensus in ethical practices. Christians can be amongst those calling most urgently for a return to former 'standards' and can equate past patterns with a kind of scriptural authority.

This would be a mistake. For when we approach social and personal morality scripturally we get neither a modern secular pattern, nor a 'traditional' one. This is true, moreover, whatever the culture. It is the case in Britain and Europe, the U.S.A. and Australia and across the continent of Africa and Asia.

I will ask the question, "What is morality?" and consider some ways in which definitions of morality have changed over the years. I shall look at what constitutes 'Traditional Morality' and the claims which were once made for a universal moral system. I shall also look at how 'contemporary morality' has repudiated these claims and produced alternative ways of living. I will conclude by suggesting that scripture must be allowed to speak into both traditional and contemporary morality. Only when scripture speaks can we move towards hope rather than disintegration.

## What is Morality?

There have been many suggestions as to how we might define morality. One is: "The provider of a reference of social order within which the human theatre is enacted." Another, offered by Edward Norman in his book *Entering the Darkness*[1] has been: "One of God's dispensations to preserve order with the societies of reasoning creatures." This suggests of course that there is no animal morality, for morality is linked with human rationality. A more prevalent definition is that morality is "a secular displacement of a religious way of life." My definition is rather more specific: 'Morality' is the outworking of a fundamental value system which directs the whole of our lives: how we relate to others, our patterns of decision-making and our response to day to day issues. Morality engages both our personal attitudes and behaviour — such as sexuality and honesty — and also the construction and behaviour of social and corporate structures, institutions and relationships.

## Changing Definitions of Morality

What counts as 'moral behaviour' has greatly changed in both social and personal spheres. When we talk about the relationship between scripture and morality we do so in the context of this change. Scripture speaks into given situations. The Bible is both itself a culturally responsive document, given in a variety of cultural contexts, and also extra cultural in that it opens up the relationship between God and the human heart at all times and eras. The norms and principles for morality which flow from scripture are themselves therefore both culturally specific and culturally transcendent. It is the job of biblical hermeneutics to help us to see which is which. (I hesitate to use the term 'culturally relative' because of the reductionist implications of the concept of relativism.)

The task of seeing morality biblically is complicated because of the shifts in morality which take place in societies. I want to address some of these changes under the very broad heading 'Traditional' and Contemporary Morality.

### Traditional Morality

Edward Norman, in his book *Entering the Darkness* makes this observation:

> The contrast with traditional societies of the past is considerable: then the passage of the season was marked by religious festivals, family life activated a discipline of devotion to the saints who would protect the members and secure their passage to eternity through intercession, public life employed religious symbolism as a signal of authority, and the extensive influence of the church maintained a visible structure of religious dedication for the purposes of human association (p. 77).

Traditional morality in Europe is in fact probably less religious than that. In the social area it centres on values such as contract-honouring, respect for authority, honouring one's parents, not lying or cheating, hard work, bravery rather than cowardice, and so on. In personal areas it would involve keeping one's word, being trustworthy, marital faithfulness, sexual integrity and so on. Traditional morality had a high view of celibacy and sexual purity and a lower view of shady dealings. In her fine novel *City of the Mind* Penelope Lively[2] sums up the remnants of traditional morality at the end of the 20th century. Her character, Matthew, had just met a thoroughly corrupt businessman and reflects on moral awareness.

> On home ground, one had been inculcated in childhood into the simple matter of sorting out right from wrong, of passing judgments. Bullies at school were to be held in contempt. You did not lie or cheat (if you did you would undoubtedly be exposed). You did not kill, steal, blaspheme, say malevolent things about people behind their backs, fiddle the income tax, torment animals, or fornicate. You were considerate of the crippled and the mentally subnormal, you gave money on flag days, you offered your seat on buses to women and elderly men. You assume that most others behaved the same, and condemned those who demonstrably did not. As you grew older you made certain adjustments to this canon (blasphemy, fornication, flag days...) but by and large it continued to condition how you behaved and expected others to behave (*City of the Mind*, p. 64).

There are some key hallmarks of European or Western traditional morality. First it was based on human respect, second it was regarded as universal — binding on everyone (including of course God in the debates of some of the eighteenth-century moralists). Thirdly, it became undergirded with an Enlightenment view of moral rationality and saw itself as self evident. The laws of morality were believed to be stamped into our human reason. Morality was therefore etched into the nature of things. (This comes over specifically in the American Declaration of Independence. Life, liberty and the pursuit of happiness were seen as *self-evident rights*, inalienable and indisputable. This is curious when one thinks of Christ's injunction not to happiness but to "take up our cross daily and follow him." We might have expected this to be reflected in the Puritan influence in the early social conditions of New England. Yet the Declaration remains a mixture of humanist and Christian ideas).

This whole concept of morality has been strongly challenged over the last few decades. It has been seen as based on many social and political ideas which robbed it of any ontological claim to universality. In particular it was seen as embodying dominant class ideas and class distinctions which often demeaned 'lower classes'. It also embodied white racial supremacy — resulting in colonialisation and patterns of disrespect. Finally, it was seen as having a ubiquitous patriarchy where men were seen as the 'norm' and women as derivations.

One of the ways in which Western traditional morality was undermined was by looking at moral systems which existed elsewhere. Soon the claim to universality disappeared. Such studies as those in New Guinea, those looking at Confucian moral systems, or those which focused on the morality derived from Islam or Hinduism weakened the popular idea in the West that their morality was universally accepted. Work done about the Nandi people of Western Kenya provided an interesting example.

## The Nandi

The Nandi live in Western Kenya, bordering the Luyia to the Ugandan border, and the Luo tribes to the south near Lake Victoria. Studies have been done on 'traditional morality' among the Nandi, especially in terms of household, marriage and work ethics. The results show that there are marked differences in how 'tradition' is interpreted between the Nandi and in Western societies.

Economically, the Nandi are pastoralists with a livelihood from cattle. The division of labour is very strict and operates from childhood along gender lines. On the whole women have traditionally cultivated the land and performed all domestic duties whilst men herded cattle and went to war. The basic organization was round the household and polygamy was accepted, especially for the well-to-do. Having more than one wife enhanced the status of men. There were, however, other strong marital taboos. Marriages between certain clans was forbidden, and within kindred groups.

Premarital sex was discouraged, especially for women. And a girl who engaged in sex before marriage was marked for life. She would be unlikely to qualify for first bride status with any partner in the future. Marriages were arranged by families, but often the first wife would advise on any future wife for her husband. Wife-wife relationships were an important part of the household arrangements and the economy.

John Rotich[3] documents how the traditional morality of the Nandi was greatly changed by a number of factors from the early part of the century. The Arab traders often took Nandi women into prostitution, and then the introduction of secular Western values also diminished traditional patterns. Greater equality between the sexes, changing work and educational ethos, and a movement away from arranged marriages were all part of the fall-out. The missionary influence because of its link with the West, played an ambiguous part in changing moral understanding. In stressing the need and centrality of 'Christian marriage' the missionaries were critically addressing some of the traditional assumptions of the Nandi. But 'Christian marriage' became itself slowly identified with white weddings, rich displays, Western customs and entry into the elite of Nandi-Western social structures. John Rotich argues that a radical scriptural morality needs to talk more about truth, faithfulness, union and communion, prayer and mutual love and submission, more than about rituals. In this sense Scripture needs to speak to both tradition and change, and even to what is perceived as 'Christian'.

## Contemporary Morality

The term 'contemporary' here is once again a very loose category. In its social context it covers all aspects of secularized individualism as well as multi-faith, materialist, and existentialist moral theories. It is not always easy to identify any clear chronological demarcation between the 'traditional' and the contemporary. As we saw from the quote from *City of the Mind* there are people in many cultures today who hold the remnants of an ethical code inherited from a previous era. These different philosophies and practices of morality, therefore, co-exist simultaneously.

Yet some hallmarks of contemporary morality break distinctly from the past. There are no insistencies that moral principles are universal and timeless. Moralities are rather contested — and seen as based on different perspectives which underlie them. The framework of commitment, or the undergirding meta-ethics give any morality its meaning. All morality relies on perspectives of interpretation or frameworks of knowledge. So, for example, on one perspective morality might be concerned with greed, theft, violence, marital breakdown, rejection of authority, corporate laziness, social conflict, law and order. On another perspective morality might be about poverty, unemployment, exploitation, deprivation, racism, sexual discrimination, inequality, lack of neighbour care. This in effect means that morality is not now seen as based in universal human rationality, but as derived from interest groups. There has also been a marked breakdown in many aspects of traditional authority. For example, as most of our newspaper headlines tell us day after day there is a determined rejection of would-be leaders. Accusations of hypocrisy, stupidity, incompetence and self interest abound. All in authority, from the British Royal Family to the Archbishop of Canterbury are regularly jeered at or 'demoted'. We could list five major shifts:

♦ There has been a breakdown in respect for people. There is a soaring crime rate with more and more violent crimes, and often now involving children as perpetrators of crime. There is fear from the elderly, as callousness and indifference to human feelings lies behind much of the heartless acts of violence. In parts of the USA, the murder rate makes some quarters of the inner city 'no-go' areas.

♦ Another growing lack is respect for truth and honesty. Fraud, computer cheating, lying, bankruptcy, illegal trading, all are part of 'normal' social relations. No longer do most people assert moral norms — e.g. 'You shall not steal', but society now concentrates on the *management* of theft. Cost of security, safeguards, anticipating when the thief might call is passed on to the rise in prices for goods.

♦ Finally in this list is breakdown of respect for families. The family has been eroded by legislation, by marital unfaithfulness, and by demanding work patterns. The effect of the Children's Act in the U.K. has yet to be fully seen.

♦ The debate has also shifted within areas of morality. No longer is there dispute about the 'big issues': sexual promiscuity, for example, or extra-marital sexual relations of any kinds. The debate now moves within those debates, to for example, the morality of AIDS testing.

♦ One other shift is that of moral discourse. There has been a marked movement from 'We' to 'I'. This is evident both in advertising, relationships and conventional therapy. But it has deeper roots. Ronald Rolheiser sums it up in his book *The Restless Heart*:[4]

> Today, we are for the most part in a *Gesellschaft* society, one characterized by the nuclear family, anonymity, and much mobility. This switch, while it has in many ways provided us with greater freedom to relate to others as we choose, has at the same time, paradoxically, helped generate and intensify loneliness by undercutting much of the interdependence which was foundational for many of our previous relationships. As we become more of a *Gesellschaft* society we seek our privacy and freedom with a passion, not wanting any interdependence forced upon us.

Morality today is undergirded by individualist values, by a materialistic commitment and a very different view of the person from that found within traditional morality or in the Biblical scripture. The result is a move further and further into the human individual becoming the arbiter of truth, meaning and social and personal decision making. Children themselves are invited increasingly to exercise their own 'rights to decide'. The pressure on the age of sexual consent illustrates the overwhelming weight put on 'choice' along with an accompanying anxiety not to over-direct such 'choice'. Within this context confusion, fear and distress are not surprising, especially amongst the young who are now expected to be mature enough to make adult moral decisions. In a context of increasing family break up and little parental guidance on how to handle conflict or understand feelings, many young people are at risk. The enormous rise of suicides amongst young people is no mere coincidence. In an era of moral confusion such an emphasis on the individual comes as hollow and empty. The resulting isolation and loneliness convey the lie that moral individualism leads to affirmation of the person. It leads rather to a society where a person's true individuality and personhood are ultimately rejected.

## Scripture and Morality

The need for the Bible to speak into our contemporary situation is crucial. The Bible must be given the freedom to speak in its own radical voice and not be shackled by the secular traditions we would want to impose on it. We need, therefore, to beware of approaching hermeneutics with our own version of moral underpinnings. Traditionalism can negate radical Biblical truth as much as any modern position. The fundamental call is rather to understand human morality in terms of a biblical view of who we are. Morality must inevitably be linked both to the doctrine of God and human personhood. Morality can never be independent of these deepest aspects of truth. Scriptural morality is not about universal rationality, or self-evident truths any more than it is about individualist self-interest or New Age pantheistic connectedness. Its starting point is not in rational autonomy, but in human creatureliness. Morality is based on our image of God and dependence on God.

Scripture then unfolds the normative structure of our lives before God and with each other. It contains principles and directions which apply to every area of life: business, marriage, work, family life, communication, sexuality, poverty and politics.

Some areas of scriptural norms can be illustrated by taking major areas of life, and asking how the Bible directs our understanding.

*Norms of neighbourliness*

There is much in scripture which can speak to the issues of property, health, wealth, land use or transport.

*Norms of honest communication*

Media, giving evidence, law courts, drama, journalism

*Norms of justice*

Law, economics, work, two-thirds world, international trade.

*Norms of compassion and care*

Vulnerable, underprivileged, sick and weak

*Norms of mercy*

In all relationships

*Norms of love, faithfulness, truth*

In personal bondings: marriage, family, friendship

Scriptural morality is never academic, but addresses human beings at the most fundamental points of their existence. It affects both the way we think; relate, act, live, and make our decisions, because it stems from our heart responses to God.

## Notes

1. Edward Norman, *Entering the Darkness* (Theale: SPCK Press, 1991).

2. Penelope Lively, *City of the Mind* (West Drayton: Penguin Books, 1992).

3. John Rotich, unpublished dissertation for Pastoral Studies, Oak Hill College, 1991.

4. Ronald Rolheiser, *The Restless Heart* (Sevenoaks: Hodder and Stoughton, 1995).

# Scripture and Social and Personal Morality
## A Response to Elaine Storkey

*Jesudasan Jeyaraj*

The hermeneutical task, proper use of the Scripture and the attitude towards God are related to the authority of Scripture and morality.

First, I agree with Dr. Elaine Storkey's view that both traditional morality and modern secular morality have certain valuable and wrong ethical principles and practices and they could be analyzed and evaluated in the light of our Christian Scripture. This is true in the case of some tribal traditional morality which usually cherish honesty, hospitality, sharing of resources and corporate responsibility. But such a traditional morality stands for the worship of nature rather than the creator, fertility cult and polygamy, sacrifices and belief in sorceries and use of spirits. Hindu morality insists on practicing charity, honesty and dharma but also encourages caste discrimination (Varnashrama system), dowry practices and inferior status of women and, recently, militancy. Modern secular morality emphasizes the protection of human rights, environment, religious freedom, welfare of women and children and communal harmony. But it has its own evils of leading the people to atheism, materialism, consumerism, individualism, ruining good ideals of traditional cultures and ignoring any authority. It is, therefore, traditional and secular morality which should be questioned and reshaped.

Dr. Elaine Storkey, however, has not argued in detail the reasons for using our Scripture to question or judge other moralities and cultures. Simply listing certain scriptural perspectives on morality, namely that there is a breadth of moral awareness within scripture and it unfolds the normative structure of our lives before God and with each other, that it contains principles and direction to every area of life and that the scriptural morality is not academic but for our existence, are not enough. The question of using our scripture to evaluate other morality and cultures is crucial to us who believe in the authority of our scripture over all moralities. People of other faiths may find fault with our scripture and reject its authority over their culture. The biblical texts which others find fault with and the questions they raise should be addressed by us. Applying the authority of our scripture over traditional or modern or theocratic culture, therefore, demands hermeneutical exercises on our side. This is a task in which some evangelical scholars should engage to show how the Christian Gospel stands in relation to other cultures and moralities.

Secondly, when we claim that our scripture can question all cultures and moralities, the ethical life of Christians is also included. In the recent years, Christian life and witness have come under the severe criticism that we are unable to show the best witness to the people of other faiths surrounding us. Although many Christians in India believe that scripture is the authority for their life and faith, they have the tendency to the selective use of the scripture, accepting certain ideals which are suitable to their vested interest and ignoring other texts which speak of justice, peace, equality and sharing. Thus they fail to relate the texts to the central message and thrust of the scripture. The way the scripture is used by Christians is another important issue related to ethical life.

Thirdly, morality not only depends upon the practice of the written scripture but also our attitude towards God. We are not merely the people of a book practising legalistic morality but the people of a personal God. Our ethical life depends upon our understanding of God. Only certain attributes of God (e.g. God is a healer, protector, blesser) to suit our convenience are emphasized. It seems in recent years, the understanding of God as holy and the need to manifest holiness in every area of our life is not emphasized very much. Isaiah's vision of God as holy needs to be kept alive among us to increase the standard of our ethical life.

# PART III
# CASE STUDIES

# Scripture in Mission

## A report of the gathering of members of the Theological Resource Network at the EFAC International Consultation, Canterbury, June 28 – July 3, 1993

*Chris Wright*

Within the overall theme of the Canterbury Consultation, "The Anglican Communion and Scripture," the specific focus of the TRN was "Scripture in Mission." Our purpose was to explore how the assumed authority of Scripture actually functions in relation to mission as it is currently practised in different contexts. Some sixteen case studies were submitted in advance and discussed in sub-groups and plenary. All continents were represented and approximately thirty members of the TRN were present.

The following report is not a statement or declaration by the TRN, but simply brings together a large number of points that emerged from the discussion of the papers. Part A summarizes several convictions that the group wished to re-affirm. Part B summarizes a wide variety of responses that were made, on the basis of the case-studies, in answer to the question "How does the Bible function in relation to mission?" Part C offers criteria which emerged as important in seeking to recognize when any mission activity may be deemed authentically biblical.

## A. The intrinsic authority of Scripture

1. We rejoice that God took the step of committing himself to

the written word and so we affirm the *intrinsic* authority of scripture as the Word of God. The authority of scripture derives from the authority of Jesus Christ as Lord and Logos. The authority of Scripture is also self-authenticating as the church tells the story of Jesus. As the Word of God, the Bible is only authoritative for the Church because it is ultimately authoritative for the whole world, as is equally true of the Lordship of Christ. Also analogously to the Lordship of Christ, the authority of the Bible as a confession of faith raises questions of historical verification, but its truth is vindicated not merely by historical research, but primarily in personal faith and obedience and will be eschatologically vindicated along with Christ.

2. We heard the challenge of African and Asian Christians to the western church to recover confidence in this authority of the Bible as Scripture, and to act upon it with more direct obedience. Without being locked into an Islamic view of scripture as simply command, the importance of obedience needs to be recovered. This matters greatly because mission only has biblical integrity when it arises out of the authentic life of the community of faith living under the authority of Scripture and when those who witness to the Gospel also demonstrate God's love and compassion. The authority of Scripture is discovered and proved in the process of obedience.

3. From Latin America we heard the challenge to develop a "critical openness" to all disciplines of human study that can throw light on the Bible and its application, including, for example, the social sciences. With proper discrimination and faithfulness to the Bible itself, we can "hold fast to that which is good" even from secular sources.

## B. The dynamic authority of Scripture

1. The functional authority of the Bible is dependent on this intrinsic authority. That is, the Bible authorizes because it is authoritative. Its function is the result of its nature as the word of God. Specifically, the Bible authorizes the church to engage in mission in God's world. As we explored the implications of the *dynamic* authority of the Bible in relation to mission, the following points were noted in related to what the Bible *does* in mission.

2. The Bible reveals the God of the whole world who seeks to draw people into fellowship with the Father through the Son, Jesus Christ, by the power of the Holy Spirit. When it is taught and applied as a whole, it keeps the church's focus on Jesus Christ as Lord and Saviour and confronts us with the whole breadth of the action and demands of the kingdom of God.

3. The Bible enables us to describe the world as God sees it, and thus to form the worldview of the believer. It exposes the sinfulness of specific human contexts and behaviour by focusing on breaches of God's laws and standards, but does so in order to motivate repentance and restoration. By studying the Bible, the Christian's mind is transformed and attitudes changed into conformity with the mind of Christ.

4. The Bible authorizes the mission of the church by providing the sole motivation, critique and destination of that mission. The Bible defines the message to be proclaimed and the lifestyle of those who proclaim it. It also provides guidance, patterns and priorities for mission in particular contexts through the richness and variety of the whole canon. The Bible also equips God's people for God's service and mission, provided it is thoroughly taught, studied and applied. This needs to be more seriously recognized as the goal of all the theological and biblical disciplines of study and teaching. The authority of the Bible for mission must be the focus of the theological education.

5. The Bible provides the basis and criteria for healthy analysis, assessment, redirection and restructuring of the church's ongoing mission. The church in mission must be constantly listening to the voice of God through his Word, in order that our mission strategy and tactics may be corrected where necessary and kept relevant to each new age and context.

6. The Bible's dynamic authority is demonstrated and validated in the transformed lives and ethical distinctiveness of Christian individuals and communities. Its power is seen in conversion, healing and deliverance.

7. The Bible empowers Christians individually and corporately to witness to Christ even in hostile contexts. The Bible vindicates the suffering of persecuted Christians as they witness to the power of the risen Christ in the eschatological hope of glory.

## C. Criteria of biblical mission

Mission may be recognized as authentically biblical:

1. When the whole canon of Scripture (Old and New Testaments) is brought to bear on mission strategy, goals and methods. Mission is biblical when it "tells the whole Bible story" and when we as individual Christians "tell our stories" in its light.

2. When the unity, clarity and integrity of Scriptures are upheld, while recognizing its diversity and complexity, in such a way that one part of the Bible is not used in contradiction to others or to legitimate an unbalanced mission strategy or method. It was also observed that through the very demands of active mission, the Holy Spirit may bring into fresh light hitherto neglected areas of the canon in each generation and context. Nevertheless, biblical mission will be recognized when its motivation, critique and destination are all provided by the canon of Scripture in its entirety.

3. When the Gospel is addressed to the whole of human life.

4. When it results in glory for the Lord Jesus Christ. For this reason, biblical mission must be Christ-centred in its motivation, consciously undertaken in obedience to Christ's command to go and make disciples, and must make known the good news of the life, death, resurrection and return of Jesus.

When it results in authentic repentance, transformation of life, and witness to Jesus as Lord, in a way which acknowledges the impact of the kingdom of God not only in the individual, but also in the community and social order. Mission thus both emerges from, and creates, communities of obedience, living witnesses to the character of God.

*The Theological Resource Network commissioned and received from its participants case studies on the use of Scripture in Mission from different contexts in the Anglican Communion. A selection of these are published with this report. The case studies were produced following a set of guidelines that were distributed. The guidelines are reproduced here since they may prove valuable for others seeking to evaluate the way that Scripture is used in the mission of their church.*

# Set of "Guidelines" for producing the Case Studies on "The Bible in Mission"

## 1. Your context

Describe the specific mission engagement that you, your church, diocese or organization are involved in. Be concise, but give as much detail as is needed for others to understand something of its social context, history, goals, methods, achievements, obstacles, problems and present situation.

## 2. Biblical authority

In what ways does your work claim biblical authority? That is, do you consciously or explicitly justify what you do in biblical terms?

Does the Bible authorize your mission work in theoretical ways (i.e., by reference to particular texts or doctrines), or in terms of biblical precedents (i.e. particular narratives or events in the Bible that you use as a norm or motivation)?

Does your mission strategy have a particular slant or thrust because of what you perceive to be a biblical priority?

Are there negative implications from your understanding of mission in the light of the Bible (i.e., things you do *not* do because you regard them as unbiblical, or not biblical priorities)?

What biblical texts, books, events or themes are dominant in your concept and practice of mission? What justifies that selection?

What hermeneutical principles, resources, tools or approaches do you respect most or find most help in practice when relating your belief in biblical authority to your practical ministry and mission?

To what extent does your context (i.e., the social-economic-political-religious realities around you) affect or control your use of the Bible; or to what extent do you critique or challenge your context from the authority of the biblical text?

## 3. Biblical distinctives

Part of Evangelicals' claim to distinctiveness is their acceptance of biblical authority. In what ways is your involvement in mission different from other possible approaches because of your view of biblical authority?

Is such biblical distinctiveness explicit in your work (e.g. is it written into your definitive documents, policy statements, etc.), or is it simply an underlying assumption?

# The Bible: Our Tool for Evangelism and Church Planting
## The Diocese of Central Tanganyika

*G. Mdimi Mhogolo*

By scratching on the surface, may I share with you some of our usage of the Bible in our evangelism and Church planting under the following headings:

- The Social and Theological Context of our Work
- Evangelism and Church Planting
- Scripture, Evangelism and Evangelists
- Scripture, Evangelism and Worship

**The Context: Social and Theological**

The Church in the Diocese of Central Tanganyika shares the social and economic sufferings of the rest of Tanzanian Society. In the context of severe economic poverty, with AIDS and malaria increasingly becoming the main killers of Tanzanians, coupled with millions of semi-literate adults, the Church becomes an open prayer to God on behalf of the whole Tanzanian society. The suffering and death of Jesus Christ becomes the point of solidarity with His Church, and His resurrection and glorification forms the basis for our hope and transformation. For us, the Cross signifies hopelessness and helplessness amidst the world's social, economic and personal sin and oppression, and the empty tomb, the hope of our victory over sin, suffering and death. The Incarnation sets the picture of our restoration and transformation, in that it brings God close to our predicament. We see God identifying himself with us. But without the Cross and the empty tomb, our hope and victory become void of power and conviction. It is in this social and theological context that the Church is active in its mission in the world — evangelism being one of the top priorities of mission in this diocese.

### Evangelism and Church Planting

Evangelism has always been the blood of the body of Christ in this diocese. However, great efforts were made in 1990 when the whole diocese focussed its attention on the neglected Kondoa district. Before we started in this area, the Diocese had 480 Christians to look after in 4 parishes. By January 1993, more than 11,000 people have been converted to Christ. We now have 18 parishes, 112 congregations which are run by 132 evangelists. For us, evangelism in the Kondoa district, which is 60% Islamic, means the sharing of the Good News to all people; converting people to Christ, resulting in the formation of congregations. Unlike the well-established churches in the diocese, these new congregations provide fellowship, care and protection to their members and show true signs of Christian community life. At the same time the congregations are very evangelistic in their approach to the mission of the Church. Whether in worship, pastoral care, Christian growth or social concern, they aim at increasing Church membership.

### Scripture, Evangelism and Evangelists

Before we send evangelists to our outreach areas we give them a two year special course which equips them with a basic biblical doctrine of salvation and skills in communication. Our evangelists are not the best theologians, but are good communicators, who believe in the Gospel, whose lives have been changed and sharpened by that same Gospel and who are keen to share the Gospel with anyone. When visiting people to bring the Good News to them, our evangelists do not go with their Bibles, which can tend to scare people away. Instead the Bible is supposed to be in their heads and hearts. Nor do they bash people with memorized verses from Scripture but use their own words and, being sensitive to the people's culture, they communicate the Good News to their audience. Moreover, our evangelists do not read pamphlets or booklets to the people, as though they have nothing in their hearts, instead they share with their audience what they believe in their hearts and minds.

As soon as people are converted to Christ our evangelists form youth choirs which put popular Scripture verse into African melodies. With the singing of these verses and dancing, they attract big crowds for open air meetings. For many the Gospel is sung and danced by believers and non-believers and its power shortly penetrates the hearts and minds of many, thus preparing a way for intensive evangelism. As soon as people are familiar with some of Jesus' teachings, we immediately move towards the preaching of the events of Jesus Christ, namely his suffering, death, his resurrection and glorification and, later on, his incarnation. We have found the solidarity and identification of Jesus with the suffering and agony of many Tanzanians more easily understood and accepted than the preaching and teaching of Jesus. People are converted to Christ not because they have been convicted by Jesus' teachings, but rather because Jesus has taken their sufferings and made them his own in order that He might help those who are still suffering and oppressed by sin, and who have not experienced the victory over all these evils. People need a saviour, a friend, a person, not a theory, a philosophy or a principle.

Sometimes people appreciate having the message communicated to them through their local languages from our playback cassettes. When we first introduced cassette ministry in the Barabaki, Wasandawi and Masai areas, it attracted huge crowds since they have never seen such a thing before. Initially, we often concentrate on the teaching of Jesus and use the art of story-telling to present examples from the Bible of people whose lives have been changed by the Gospel. We sometimes use "problem-solving" methods in trying to introduce Christ to them. Our approach is always practical and must be realistic to the lives of our audience. The virtues of caring, hospitality and social concern are highly recommended. A network of support groups has been established through linking a new parish with established deaneries. Every year people from deaneries visit their link parishes for sharing, helping them in their witness, praying together and supporting them financially and materially. Non-believers have frequently noticed "Look, how they love each other." We see all this as biblically based and inspired and we try to live today as the early Church did yesterday.

### Scripture, Evangelism and Worship

Christians are still regarded as the people of the Book. Since many of our Christians are illiterate, or semi-literate, we have developed forms of worship which do not depend heavily on reading skills. We have to respond to peoples' hearing and seeing rather than reading. As the people have no "Christian" symbolism to help them in worship, we always have to try to encourage people to have new approaches, feelings and responses through music and dancing in their worship of God. We always have to be conscious of the presence of God in their environment and culture so that the God of our Lord Jesus may be the God of their environment and culture. We have found prayer and intercession, including exorcism, the healing of diseases, mental, psychological and spiritual, have proved the only effective ways to introduce Jesus Christ as Lord, Saviour and Friend. God, in action, through Jesus Christ has been able to be their Lord and Friend in their own environment. For this reason, people have been able to worship God, singing his praises and dancing before him, as they celebrate the Eucharist; a comfort for their needy souls.

When Scripture is read and preached to these young congregations, we normally select narrative passages and the stories of Jesus Christ from the Gospels. Preaching consists of retelling of the stories with simple application to their daily living. We have found the doctrines of the epistles are hard for most of these young Christians to understand. We believe as people become used to different concepts of truths of the Bible and become more versatile in reading that they will be able to understand the truths of the epistles. If only we could paraphrase the epistles we would help speed up the maturity of these young Christians!

### Conclusion

For us, the authority of the Bible is seen in its power to change peoples' lives and strengthen our understanding of our world. The power of Scripture is not seen in its practical theories and philosophies, but resides in a God who acts and is involved in the affairs of the world. Scripture points to God who becomes known and loved and worshipped by those people who have been converted to him through Jesus Christ. When people obey the truths of Scriptures they do so, not for the sake of the truth per se, but instead in obeying the truth, they obey God.

# Proverbial, Intrinsic and Dynamic Authorities
## Scripture and Mission in the Dioceses of Mount Kenya East and Kirinyaga

*Graham Kings*

## Introduction

... we doubt whether it will be possible for Europeans to live always in the Highlands. And when these settlers, who are strong, however powerful they may be, wish to take away the lands of the Black people for their own benefit in their own interests, we remember the matter of Ahab when he took Naboth's vineyard.[1]

This was written in 1928 in the third edition of a radical Kikuyu monthly newsletter, *Muigwithania* (newsbearer, reconciler, unifier). It was edited by Johnstone Kenyatta who later became the first President of Kenya.

The 140 acres of cattle holding ground at Sagana have been reverted to other use. We have information that one powerful individual has grabbed 60 acres of that land for his own use and some of his supporters have also received a share of this public land. And there was no Naboth to say No![2]

This was preached in 1991, by David Gitari, Bishop of Kirinyaga. I was in the congregation that day, together with students from St. Andrew's Institute Kabare where I had been on the staff since 1985, and remember the electric atmosphere of that Bible exposition.

Sixty-three years separated these differing applications against British colonialists and Kenyan neo-colonialists. Both Kenyatta and Gitari were Kikuyu; both used the scriptural story of I Kings 21. Their attitude to scriptural authority however was different.

Kenyatta alluded to the story which would have been known to his readers through preaching.[3] It is interesting that he uses the Scriptures against the white people who brought the Scriptures. It seems to me to be unlikely that he viewed that story as "the Word of God" but it was certainly useful for his purpose. He may have considered the story to have "proverbial authority" for Kikuyu proverbs often mention only the main character of a traditional story and the rest is inferred. Perhaps this is an example of someone who does not seem to have been a committed Christian, who uses Scripture for a biblically just purpose, though with traditional "proverbial authority."[4]

Gitari, however, is a regular expository preacher, in the evangelical tradition[5] and in his sermon in 1991 he more than alluded to the story of Naboth: he expounded it in depth. He holds a very high doctrine of Scripture's "intrinsic authority" as God's Word combined with an imaginatively shrewd, political acumen. For him, the story of Naboth's vineyard had the "intrinsic authority" of God's Word and the "dynamic authority" of God's prophetic Word for that day. To see the background to his, and others', use of Scripture in mission we need to outline the context.

## Context

Gitari was the first and last Bishop of the Diocese of Mount Kenya East. This stretched from the fertile agricultural land just south of Mount Kenya up to the deserts near the Ethiopian border. In 1990, after 15 years of extraordinary growth,[6] the diocese died and rose again into two dioceses: Kirinyaga, led by Bishop Gitari, and Embu led by Bishop Moses Njue who had served as a missionary to West Germany for 5 years.

Before Independence in 1963 the British colonial government had exercised the policy of "divide and rule." Between 1975 and 1990 the diocesan mission strategy had been one of "divide and grow"! Five year development plans, arising out of Partnership in Mission Consultations, aimed at dividing parishes by particular dates, for example, a parish of 6 congregations would divide into two parishes of 3, which would then plant more congregations. On this model deaneries and archdeaconries would divide and this eventually led to the division of the diocese. This growth was based on the integration of evangelism, development and action for social justice.[7]

In several sermons and addresses Gitari developed his theology of mission on the basis of Luke 2:52. He applied the words about Jesus growing in wisdom and stature, in favour with God and people to his desire that every child in the diocese should also have such an opportunity for mental, physical, spiritual and social growth. Therefore the diocesan mission strategy included the involvement in education, community health work, evangelism and social transformation.[8]

President Moi took over from Kenyatta on the latter's death in 1978. Moi is an evangelical Christian who is, however, very wary of the application of the Bible to social ethics. During the 1980's he increasingly tightened his grip on the one party state, with consequential human rights abuses, but was forced by international pressure to allow multiparty democracy in November 1991.[9] A local cabinet minister, James Njiru, was the Ahab referred to in May 1991. He had set up two "front" companies called Kariko Jaken Tree Nurseries and Jimka Developers and Lodges Company. Having sketched the background, let us return to the sermon preached in May 1991.

### Was there no Naboth to say No?

The service itself, on Rogation Day, was outside the Church at Mutuma, on the southern slopes of Mount Kenya, actually overlooking Kamuruana Hill which had already been grabbed and shaved of trees. It looked bald! For his sermon, Gitari had worked on some detailed research not only of the text but of the context. During the sermon, after a long exegetical retelling of the Naboth story, he read out the minutes he had obtained of the local council town planning committee for 19 February 1991.[10]

It was agreed that:

The ten acre plot for the establishment of a tree nursery at

Kamuruana Hill be allocated to Kariko Jaken Tree Nurseries.

An application for a motel site at Kamuruana Hill by Jimka Developers and Lodges Company was considered and approved.

Gitari preached "of the 16 Councillors who met, there was not a single one with the courage of Naboth to say No" and added this refrain after each detailed accusation of land grabbing. Later on he anticipated the attacks of politicians on him in the words of Ahab and turned the tables on them:

> In an earlier story when Elijah emerged from hiding, King Ahab greeted him with the words "Is that you, you troubler of Israel?" (I Kings 18:17). That greeting poses a big question. Who is the troubler of Israel? The prophet or the King? And in today's Kenya, the people who cause trouble are not necessarily the Bishops.
>
> Who are the troublers in Kenya? They are the land grabbers, the election riggers, those who sit in Councils and know what is wrong and have no courage to say No!
>
> The troublers of Kenya are those who wish to put the clock back so that we can revert to *mlolongo*.[11]
>
> The troublers of Kenya are those who plan transfers of civil servants who do not support them politically thus causing innocent people to suffer for nothing.[12]
>
> The troublers of Kenya are those who plan to send thugs to raid homes of people at night.[13]

The sermon ended with a plea for repentance and the consequent assurance of God's forgiveness.

So this is a fascinating example of directing the living Words of God (which, as Luther used to say, "have hands and feet") to contemporary issues of justice. It was powerful because of its detailed retelling and because the congregation knew the context and political references.

### Scriptural Litany for the Environment

The sermon was followed up with a creative Litany for the Environment. The Bishop had phoned the Institute the previous

Friday and asked the students to produce a litany for the Sunday. The morning was transformed as students searched concordances for references to trees, fields, cedars, etc. and dug deep into the background of the passages thus found. Eventually a catena of scriptural passages was set out in dramatic form with various readers as well as versicles and responses by the Bishop and people.[14]

The litany, apart from the final lines, was deliberately made up only of Scriptural quotations. Its first section was headed Celebration of Creation and had verses from Psalms 24:1-2, 104:16-17 and 24:3-4. The second was headed Judgment on Those Who Destroy the Environment and contained verses from the book of Isaiah (Is. 5:20-21, 13:2, 3:14-15, 5:8-9, 10:1-2, 37:23-24, 37:29). The following were originally directed against Sennacherib:

Reader:     By your servants you have mocked the Lord,
            and you have said, "With many chariots
            I have gone up the heights of the mountains,
            to the far heights of Lebanon;
            I felled its tallest cedars,
            I came to its remotest height,
            its densest forest.

                                                    (Isaiah 37:24)

Bishop:     Thus says the Lord,

Reader:     "Because you have raged against me
            and your arrogance has come to my ears,
            I will put my hook in your nose
            and my bit in your mouth,
            and will turn you back on the way
            by which you came."

                                                    (Isaiah 37:29)

The final section was headed Hope for Creation and had verses from Job 15:7-9, Psalm 96:12-13, Isaiah 14:5 and 8, 55:12.

Reader:     The pine trees and the cedars of Lebanon exult
            over you and say,

People:     "Now that you have been laid low,
            no woodsman comes to cut us down."

                                                    (Isaiah 14:8)

| Bishop: | For you shall go out in joy,<br>and be led forth in peace;<br>and the mountains and the hills before you<br>shall break forth into singing, |
|---|---|
| People: | and all the trees of the field<br>shall clap their hands. |

(Isaiah 55:12).

Again the Scriptures were used imaginatively, and with performative force, but with discernment. They were not just a quarry for pertinent texts, for not every passage that was suggested, on deeper study, shed light on the current context. They were alive with resonances across the years and lands.

### Daniel Chapter 6 and Kenya Today?

In June 1987 biblical interpretation was debated in Parliament, in the newspapers and, more importantly, on *matatus* (small private buses/vans) throughout Kenya! Did Daniel chapter 6 apply to Kenya today? Gitari had preached that it did: David Amayo, the chairman of KANU (the one political party), insisted that it did not:

> Bishop Gitari's biblical reference to the book of Daniel chapter 6, about Darius and Daniel, has no parallel in Kenya. Such comparison can only be made with the aim of confusing God-fearing and peace-loving Kenyans.[15]

In June 1987 Gitari preached four expository sermons which focussed on issues of social justice and caused this national debate. These were later published, together with the press cuttings of political reaction. This was the third sermon, on 21 June, and was preached at a civic service in St. Peter's Church, Nyeri, with the District Commissioner, the Mayor, the Chairman of the County Council and the local Party Chairman in the congregation.

In the recent past a prominent Kenyan civil servant had been sacked and in August 1986 a KANU resolution to institute the unconstitutional system of voting by queuing up behind photos of candidates had been hastily passed. There was an outcry from the churches and lawyers and then public debate on "queuing" had been quashed.

After setting the context of Daniel 6 in the Persian Empire with the plot to remove Daniel, the loyal and just civil servant, Gitari referred to the change in the Persian constitution which brought this about:

> In Persia the king approved the change in the constitution without any debate. The greatest mistake we can make in our national life is to allow important decisions to be made without allowing sufficient time for all those concerned to debate the issues...

> Because the king did not allow a public debate, he was caused to make a blunder which he greatly regretted. The rulers of this world should be extremely careful of those advisers who claim to be loyal to the king while at the same time plotting to undermine efficient, capable and honest servants of the king.[16]

Since politicians and others were debating the biblical interpretation of Daniel 6 that week, the following Sunday Gitari preached on 2 Timothy 3:14-4:7 under the title "All Scripture is Inspired by God"(!). After exegetical detail on the background, Gitari continued:

> There is not one bit of scripture that is useless even for the present generation. When the Bible says that "all" scripture is profitable it means exactly that; it is every part of the Bible which is profitable. But now the Chairman of KANU, speaking on behalf of our beloved party, has come forward to tell us what is not profitable in the scriptures ... As far as we preachers are concerned, all scripture including Daniel 6 is profitable for every generation and is profitable for Kenya today.[17]

Later on he commented on the phrase "in season and out of season":

> Has any politician a right to tell a preacher when it is convenient to preach on certain issues and when it is inconvenient? If I have to choose between what a politician tells me and what St. Paul commends, I will take the side of the Apostle.[18]

Gitari's public use of the Scriptures to back up his earlier use of the Scriptures shows a confidence in their authority and power to highlight and correct social injustice.

## A Kenyan Passion Play

In 1991 as an evangelistic drama, two students at St. Andrew's Institute Kabare, Pauline Njiru and Albert Kabiro, wrote a Kenyan Passion play. This was the last week of Jesus' life with echoes of the current events and political language of Kenya.[19]

Part of it was performed on Graduation Day, 12 October 1991. In August 1990, the prophetic Bishop Muge had been threatened by Peter Okondo, a Cabinet minister, that if he went to Busia he "would see fire and may not leave alive." He went and died. A lorry smashed into his car on the way home. On Graduation Day, a shiver went through the crowd when Jesus was warned by the Sadducees: "If you go to Jerusalem, you will see fire and may not leave alive."

Another politician, Shariff Nassir from Mombasa, caused a stir when he said that the queuing system of voting would be implemented "whether the people like it or not." In Kiswahili this neat catch phrase *"wapende wasipende"* became infamous. In the Passion Play the scene portraying the Sanhedrin Council, deciding the fate of Jesus, concluded with the High Priest saying this: "I know the people are behind him, but we will have to get rid of him — *wapende wasipende"*. A gasp went up in the crowd.

## Conclusion

This case study has looked at episcopal sermons and student litanies and drama to consider the use of Scripture in mission in the dioceses of Mount Kenya East and of Kirinyaga.

The use outlined here seems to me to be not so much the facile twisting of Scripture to catch people's attention but a profound resonance of the living Word in a later age and culture which has echoes of prophetic, political reinterpretations: perhaps like the book of Daniel itself in the second century BC and the book of Revelation in the first century AD? This is more than the "proverbial authority" we saw at the beginning, for Scripture is recognized in its "intrinsic authority" as the Word of God and, since it is alive, it has contemporary "dynamic authority" in life and in death.

We have concentrated on the application of Scripture to social and political issues: however, the "dynamic authority" that Scripture carries in these various situations is partly due to the fruits of evangelism in the diocese. Since there are so many Christians who revere the Bible and who are politically aware, if a particular application of Scripture is valid then it does have social and political consequences. This practical "dynamic authority," which is based on "intrinsic authority," and which flourishes in an environment of a growing Church with perceptive insights, will be worth exploring further.

## Notes

1. Kikuyu Central Association, *Muigwithania*, vol. 1 (3) July 1928, p. 7. Cited in John Karanja, *The Growth of the African Anglican Church in Central Kenya, 1900-1945* (Cambridge Ph.D. dissertation) 1993, p. 162.

2. David Gitari, "Was There No Naboth to Say No?" (p. 8) Duplicated sermon script of a sermon preached at Trinity Church Mutuma, Kenya on 19 May 1991 on the occasion of a Diocesan Environmental Service.

3. The Kikuyu Old Testament translation was not issued till 1951, though the Kiswahili Old Testament translation, which some of his readers would have known, was issued in 1915.

4. Later he seems to have misused Scripture and subverted an African Independent Church partly through substituting the name Jomo Kenyatta (J.K.) for Jesu Kristo in its hymn books! See L.S.B. Leakey, *Defeating Mau Mau* (London: Methuen, 1954) cited in the review of the book by Leonard Beecher, "After Mau Mau – What?" *International Review of Missions* XLIV, No. 174 (1955): 205-211. Beecher continues (p. 207): "Even the National Anthem had few words substituted for the well-established Kikuyu version; these new words enabled the followers of Kenyatta to sing loudly and fervently in support of sedition whenever loyal subjects of the Queen stood to pray God's blessing on her Majesty when the National Anthem was sung."(!)

5. Before being consecrated Bishop, Gitari had been the General Secretary of the Bible Society of Kenya and before theological studies in England had been an evangelist in African Universities. At the 1988 Lambeth Conference he was Chairman of the Resolutions Committee.

6. The following statistics bear witness to this phenomenal growth: between 1975 and 1990 the parishes rose from 19 to 93, the numbers of vicars rose from 30 to 120, of Deaconesses from 0 to 20, of Community Health Workers from 0 to 308. 67 Church buildings were consecrated, including Embu Cathedral, about 150,000 people were baptized and about 90,000 confirmed. 2 missionaries were sent to other countries, to Zaire and West Germany.

7. See D. Gitari, "Evangelization and Culture" in V. Samuel and A. Hauser (eds.), *Proclaiming Christ in Christ's Way: Studies in Integral Evangelism* (Oxford: Regnum, 1989), pp. 101-121.

8. For further details see Grace Gitari, "Evangelical Development in Mount Kenya East," *Transformation* 5, no. 4 (1988): 44-46.

9. For further details see D. Gitari, "Church and Politics in Kenya," *Transformation* 8, no. 3 (1991): 7-17.

10. D. Gitari, "Was There No Naboth to Say No?" (p. 6). This sermon is amongst twenty-five of David Gitari's sermons given between 1975 and 1994 published by Regnum Africa under the title *In Season and Out of Season*, Akropong 1996. Further details from Regnum Africa at the Akrofi-Christaller Memorial Centre, P O Box 76, Akropong-Akuapem, Ghana or Regnum Books International, P O Box 70, Oxford OX2 6HB, UK.

11. The Kikuyu for the "Queuing system" of voting which Moi instated in 1986 for preliminary elections and which was open to massive rigging. Moi was forced by pressure from the churches and the people to abandon the system at the end of 1990.

12. This may refer to Simon Nyachae, a former head of the civil service who had previously been sacked.

13. This refers to the attempted assassination of Gitari in April 1989 by thugs. It was considered by most local people that Njiru was behind this attempt: there was a Presidential Commission of Enquiry, but the results have been concealed.

14. The full text was published in *News of Liturgy*, August 1991: 8-10.

15. *Daily Nation* June 27, 1987 cited in D. Gitari, *Let the Bishop Speak* (Nairobi: Uzima, 1989), p. 40.

16. D. Gitari, *Let the Bishop Speak* (Nairobi: Uzima, 1989), pp. 36-37.

17. Ibid., pp. 45-46.

18. Ibid., p. 47.

19. See also John V Taylor "The Development of African Drama for Education and Evangelism," *International Review of Missions* XXXIV, no. 55 (1950): 292-301.

20.

# A Biblical Vision for Diocesan Life

## The Diocese of St Mark the Evangelist
## (Province of Southern Africa)

*Philip Le Feuvre*

One of my fellow-bishops, in a discussion concerning the Decade of Evangelism, commented, "I don't want a whole bunch of fundamentalists thumping around my Diocese." To which another bishop responded, "I don't think fundamentalism is our problem. Our problem is people who don't know their Bibles at all."

This is a remarkably accurate assessment of the Diocese of St. Mark the Evangelist, a diocese in the far northern Transvaal, which, while having a large number of long-established and settled congregations, mainly rural, is dedicated chiefly to the ministry of primary evangelism, discipleship and church-planting. The largest number of unevangelized people remaining in the Republic of South Africa live in this Diocese, where, an added evangelistic incentive, 70 percent of the population is under twenty-five.

Curiously and sadly enough, it is often the long-established congregations that constitute a real obstacle to the Diocese's evangelistic goals. There is a high degree of formalism and traditionalism, in which, in many cases, evangelism itself is regarded as 'un-Anglican', an undesirable and interfering activity indulged in by the independent churches and other less reputable sects. That the Lambeth fathers should have declared a Decade of Evangelism is often regarded with some bewilderment, coupled with a strong determination to have as little to do with it as possible. There is a nominal agreement that some attention should be given to young people, but mainly because their elders see this an antidote to disobedience in the home, sexual promiscuity, and alcohol and drug abuse. Our congregations — and certainly our councils — are thoroughly middle-aged, firmly of the opinion that the young people should be present, but should know their place.

Lest you should feel that these are the outpourings of a bishop grown cynical by bitter disillusion, let me hasten to add that there are notable exceptions to this overall picture. It is precisely in one of the most unevangelized areas that the congregations, assisted by workers from the Diocese of Singapore, have been wonderfully empowered by the Holy Spirit to reach out into neighbouring communities, to win whole families for Christ, and to disciple them within the context of house-groups and newly planted congregations. In other parts of the Diocese, too, there have been both individuals and small groups of people who have "stumbled upon" the biblical vision of a growing church, of gospel-permeated communities, of changed lives. They struggle to find a way for this vision to be translated into reality in their parishes, but often against staunch opposition.

The difference is — the Bible! The tradition of the Diocese is one in which ownership of the prayer-book and hymn-book has been exalted above that of the Bible, and in which the proper ordering of the liturgy has taken precedence over its biblical content. And woe be to him/her who fiddles with that! (I was severely hauled over the coals by church wardens for saying "Hallelujah! The Lord is here", when 'the book' said simply, "The Lord is here.") It is significant that, wherever there has been an upsurge of evangelism and spiritual life, it has been accompanied by a rediscovery of the word of God and a determination to do what it says. If there is anything which encourages me in the Diocese at the moment, it is a turning (yes, in many places, only slight, but in others considerable) towards a more biblically-based preaching and teaching.

## The Subiaco Vision

It was a sense amongst some that the Holy Spirit was beginning to move in this way, despite all obstacles and discouragements, that led the Diocesan Finance Board (of all unlikely bodies!) to ask for the convening of a small four-day conference to pray, wait upon the Lord, study the Scriptures together and find the direction in which he wanted the Diocese to move. The result was the Subiaco Vision (named after the Roman Catholic monastery at which the conference was held):

"From 11-13 May 1992, a Diocesan Strategy Planning Conference, chaired by a leading Christian strategist from Johannesburg, took place near Pietersburg (at the Subiaco Monastery). It was an extremely exciting event, and I want to tell you something of it and of the decisions that were made. We began with the firm conviction that God was talking to us from Exodus 25:8-9.

Make me a sanctuary and I shall dwell among the Israelites. Make it exactly according to the design I show you.

We believe that God wants this Diocese to become a place in which God dwells among His people, and we started by asking Him to show us what His design for us is. And we believe He did so.

I could go into a great amount of detail, and doubtless I shall do some of that as I move around the Diocese meeting Parish and Chapelry Councils. But the broad outlines are as follows:

1. What is the Sanctuary God wants us to build?

It is a Diocese —

(a) made up of parishes in which there is trained leadership, God-centred and lively worship, evangelism, teaching, loving service, and active young people;

(b) staffed by relevantly trained clergy involved in relevant ministry;

(c) providing for its own human and financial needs;

(d) ministering to the needs of needy communities and people;

(e) run along the lines shown us by the Lord.

2. And what are these lines? What is His design?

(a) That fewer decisions should be taken in the Diocesan Office, and more at the Archdeaconry level;

(b) That there will be a committee, to advise the Bishop in keeping this vision on track;

(c) Each Archdeacon along with two Lay representatives from each Archdeaconry will form a special body to advise the Bishop;

(d) That in every Archdeaconry there will be an Archdeaconry Trainer, who will be responsible, alongside TFM, for the training of community clergy, i.e., non-stipendiary, lay ministers and congregations in that Archdeaconry. He/she will give courses and workshops especially on ministry, worship, evangelism and discipleship.

(e) That full-time ministers and clergy will no longer be paid by the Diocese but by the parishes themselves directly;

(f) That, instead of the laity in the parishes helping the clergy in their job, the clergy will help the laity in theirs. Community clergy will take over more and more sacramental responsibilities, freeing the full-time clergy for teaching and other specialist ministries. The laity will be more and more responsible for pastoral ministry.

(g) There will be a full-time youth pastor in every parish;

(h) There will be a Diocesan committee to monitor and arrange ministry in cases of special community need (e.g., drought, famine, refugees).

The object of these changes is to free the Bishop for a greater participation in the teaching ministry for which he was consecrated, and to put responsibilities for ministry and the making of important decisions into the hands of the people in the parishes and Archdeaconries. We want to see the Diocese come alive in the power of the working of God's Holy Spirit in every place, a Sanctuary for God to dwell in. Please pray for it."

This vision has since been adopted officially by Diocesan Synod. The Diocesan Administrator and I have been visiting all the parishes individually in order to explain the vision in detail, to share our expectations, to try to get everybody as excited as we are, but also to make no secret of the fact that it does lay upon the parish cost and responsibility. Some are frankly cynical; for some the cost is too high — or so they say (it does require some degree of faith for a parish, when it cannot even afford its own priest, to think in terms of a full-time youth-pastor plus 25 percent of the cost of an archdeaconry teacher-trainer); but in many other places the belief has been asserted that this can work, that it is from God, and that therefore He will provide what is necessary.

What has been achieved thus far? A committee, representative of all archdeaconries, to advise me is in place. So is one archdeaconry teacher-trainer, thanks once again to the Diocese of Singapore, and a second is due in January 1994, thanks this time to Crosslinks. I believe that the structure has got to be sustained from within the Diocese — and will be — but the Lord's help to us through Singapore and Crosslinks has enabled us to move more quickly than would otherwise have been possible. Most parishes are now paying their clergy directly, and not giving reluctantly through the unwelcome anonymity of the Diocese. This has increased motivation in giving in most places (not all!) where it is being applied, but a legal contract has had to be drawn up in order to protect all parties. One parish is looking to appointing a youth-pastor, but this is a costly item, and most parishes are afraid of it. I believe that in our context it is probably the most vital of all recommendations, but I also believe that, if we are faithful, the Lord will lead us into that one in His time. There is now a very effective Diocesan crisis committee handling both relief and development issues which has been able to channel aid and ministry to drought victims and Mozambican refugees (there are over 120,000 in the diocese, and we can do less than scratch the surface with our limited resources, but we believe that in this area we have been obedient).

### A Biblical Assessment

I am the first bishop of a Diocese that came into being in 1987. This raised two questions for me: what were to be the priorities of my ministry as a bishop, and what was the Lord's intention for this new Diocese? The two questions were clearly linked.

In response to the first question, especially in a Diocese as unevangelized as St. Mark the Evangelist, I felt that the Holy Spirit was laying on me more and more the apostolic emphases of prayer, the ministry of the word (Acts 6:4) and a concern for all the congregations (2 Corinthians 11:28), their creation and their growth. Instead, I found myself encumbered with administration, correspondence and endless confirmations of ill-prepared candidates. Doubtless the apostolic emphases can — and must — be exercised in all of these, but it did not seem to me quite what Scripture was saying.

The purpose for which the Province had brought the Diocese into being was to promote evangelism and church growth. This seems to me eminently right — the whole context seems to justify a Pauline strategy of evangelism (Acts 26:19-21, 1 Corinthians 2:1-5), discipling (2 Corinthians 11:2), the defining and growth of koinonia (1 Corinthians 12, Ephesians 4-6), the development and training of leadership (Acts 14:23; 20:18-35), the fostering of stewardship (2 Corinthians 8, 9; 1 Corinthians 12), and continuing to remember the poor (Galatians 2:10). This is not just accidental. More and more it has seemed to the leadership of the Diocese that the Pauline pattern is the one to follow, and this is reflected in the Subiaco vision. While there is the necessity of maintaining an apostolic leadership in ministry and doctrine, it would seem thoroughly biblical to give to each congregation a sense of identity in the Lord, resulting in the experience of that fellowship that shares, ministers to one another and reaches out with a degree of autonomy that is tempered by the local situation. This is what is presupposed and outlined in every congregation to which Paul wrote.

A grasp of 'apostolic doctrine', of the teaching of Scripture, is precisely what is lacking in and what is enervating the activity of so many congregations in the Diocese. The inability to understand the central importance of the word of God, let alone to be living in conformity with it, is what needs to be addressed at a pastoral level ("Our problem is people who don't know their Bibles at all") — and this, surely, is the motivation that lies behind the writing of the whole New Testament. It was to teach, so that those who learn might teach others also (2 Timothy 2:2). Again and again we hear repeated in the Diocese that there never has been and is no adequate teaching of the people. This is now a priority.

This, under the Holy Spirit, will lead to the empowering of the whole people of God, as is clearly envisaged by the New Testament. It is therefore essential that as thorough a programme of teaching as possible should be embarked on in the Diocese, and that it should be undertaken by people who have total faith in the Bible as the authentic word of God. So many of the clergy at present ministering in the Diocese were trained under a negative scholarship that, if not directly, at least by powerful implication questioned the authority of the Scripture. No wonder, then, that their preaching is half-hearted and lacking conviction, and their congregations inadequately instructed. Our present ordinands must be trained in an environment in which Scripture is honoured, well taught and presented to enable the full-time clergy to devote their ministries to biblical living, teaching and pastoral activity. Those to whom special teaching responsibilities in the Diocese are entrusted must be men and women who feel themselves commissioned to pass on the apostolic tradition, which is, after all, the New Testament (which, in its turn, is the Old interpreted in the light of the Christ-event). This alone can be the basis for healthy church growth, the development of leadership and the spiritual formation of individual Christian men and women (Acts 20:32, 2 Timothy 3:14-17).

Another key emphasis is the concept of the laity having the primary ministry function in the congregation, with the clergy preparing and training them to fulfil this function (Ephesians 4:11-13). Today this emphasis in the New Testament, 'every-member ministry', is widely recognized and encouraged, but that is not the same thing as seeing it practised. Where the biblical base of a congregations's perceptions, insights and expectations is thin and where its understanding of the role of the clergy is purely professional, every-member ministry will be either resisted as an innovation or honoured in the breach but not in the execution.

And that leads me back to my first question: what is the role of the bishop in all this? While unbiblical patterns remain, it will continue to be a largely unproductive round of administration, correspondence and confirmations. Administration and correspondence cannot be eliminated altogether — the latter half of the New Testament is virtually all correspondence, and much of it touches on administration. What will change is the productiveness of it. For when this is being exercised and fed into a context of truly biblical church-life patterns, it is received and taken up in a way which furthers the preaching of the gospel, the teaching of discipleship and the growth of the Kingdom. And behind it all will lie the expertise and reality of the bishop as a person who is dedicated to the word of God and prayer, which he has now been set free to do.

I, as a bishop, have inherited certain patterns of ministry which are of long-standing and have created definite expectations of both clergy and bishop by the people. It has also led them into a very minimal concept of their own role, a concept that, strangely enough, they are not always keen to change. This pattern has many and mixed origins: an undue emphasis on sacrament and ritual, an erroneous concept of priesthood and episcopacy, a loss of confidence in the authority and relevance of Scripture, the devaluing of evangelism in favour of a mission described purely in political, economic and social terms. Sacrament, ministry and diakonia are all essential to the life and witness of the Church, but the balance is set for us by Scripture, and the Bible's priorities must be ours. There are many forces at work in the world which seek to push up into the direction of emphasizing some things over others in a way which Scripture does not warrant. In Scripture God has communicated to us His perspectives; in ministry they must be ours also.

# Mission Policies: The Result of Bible Reading or the Result of Circumstances?

## St. Mary Overchurch (Upton), Diocese of Chester, England

*Paddy Benson*

How does the Bible shape our mission?

As evangelicals, we want our mission to be directed by God speaking through Scripture. However it seems that in reality the shape of our mission is dictated by external circumstances before we ever open our Bibles.

The parish where I work as a curate, St. Mary's Upton in the Diocese of Chester, England is a case in point. The church's mission has altered in recent years, but we can identify important non-biblical factors which have compelled the changes.

### The Change in St. Mary's Mission

#### St. Mary's Upton

St Mary's is reputed as a large and flourishing evangelical Anglican church. On an ordinary Sunday, about 600 adults and 150 children attend services and classes. These numbers are slightly lower than fifteen years ago, although there is a steady trickle of new converts.

Expository preaching and Bible study have been of central

importance in St. Mary's for more than thirty years, both in church services and in home group meetings. The church is committed to discovering God's will in Scripture, and putting it into practice. Despite the appearance of continuity and stability, St Mary's mission has altered during the last ten years. Three factors have contributed to this alteration.

### First factor: 'competition' from other churches

St Mary's grew from a small local church to its present size during the time of the previous vicar, Roy Barker (incumbent 1962-1980). At that time St Mary's was one of only two such evangelical Anglican churches on the Wirral peninsula. Anglican evangelicals travelled in to St Mary's from the surrounding communities: many from West Kirby, Meols and Heswall (five miles away); some from as far as North Wales, thirty miles or more. St Mary's eclectic congregation was largely middle-class: business people and professionals such as doctors.

In 1982 Michael Baughen, a leading evangelical, became Bishop of Chester. The new bishop encouraged evangelical clergy to take up positions of responsibility in his diocese. Within a few years St. Mary's was surrounded by numerous other Bible-centred ministries; while other parishes whose incumbents were not evangelical nevertheless became more accommodating to evangelicals. St Mary's began to notice the change: evangelical Anglicans no longer needed to travel long distances to Upton in order to hear clear biblical preaching, and St Mary's congregations began to shrink.

Under the present incumbent, Nigel Walker, St. Mary's has understood this as God's call to concentrate on the parish of Upton: that is, instead of being a church for a middle-class *network*, it has to become a church for the Upton *neighbourhood*.

### Second factor: the need to cross social boundaries

The first factor had compelled St. Mary's to change its *missiology*. Instead of reaching out to those who are nearby socially, it was forced to concentrate on those nearby geographically. But at once St. Mary's faced a problem. The parish is socially very mixed: some areas of expensive housing, but other streets of smaller houses of artisans, and also large estates with high unemployment. The congregation looked intimidating and mid-dle-class to the majority of the parish: even those who wanted to respond to the gospel found it difficult to feel at home in the church.

St. Mary's made its services more accessible to a wider range of people. However it recognized that the present church and its services would never be adequate as the focus of mission and outreach to the whole parish. It had to change its *ecclesiology*. As well as its parish church, St. Mary's needed other congregations which were geographically and socially nearer to the people.

The first new congregation, 'St Mary's Centre', meets in two adjacent shops which the church has bought at one edge of the parish. It draws much of its congregation from a nearby de-pressed estate. A second new congregation is planned in a school hall on the opposite side of the parish. Eventually we hope to have a string of satellite congregations in various locations. The satellites will have their own identities. Their leadership will reflect the majority community in their area. Their style of wor-ship and other meetings will be dictated by the culture and needs of the other particular people who worship there. Yet although each satellite is a focus of Sunday morning worship and mid-week activities, its members are encouraged to come to the parish church for a central service on Sunday night. This is an opportu-nity for Christians from the whole parish to come together in celebration, as the parish's unity in Christ is expressed, despite all its social diversity.

The pattern of numerous small congregations has an implica-tion for ministry. At present, clergy participate in small services, but as the congregations multiply the clergy role becomes one of oversight of the predominantly lay leadership.

### *Third factor: outreach beyond the church fringe*

In May 1993 a South African visitor to the parish, Revd. David Selane, addressed a class at a local secondary school. He asked the class how many of them attended any church. Not a single member of the class, nor their teacher, attended a church, al-though one girl said she had done so when she was younger.

This experience illustrates a fact which recent studies have

disclosed, namely the shrinkage of the church's 'fringe' membership — that is, people who are not active church members but
are nevertheless linked to a church and have some knowledge of
Christian teaching. The vast majority of English children, 86
percent, have never attended a Sunday School or had any other
church link.

As St. Mary's concentrated on its neighbourhood instead of
its old network, it began to feel the force of this statistic. Its new
mission field in the artisan housing and the large estates included
many people who were economically poor and also completely
unchurched. Outreach among such people brought new priorities in our pastoring and preaching.

The unchurched parts of Upton experience problems that the
middle-class, partly churched network does not have in the same
measure — or perhaps they were just cleverer at hiding them.
On the large housing estates, St. Mary's confronts the daily
reality of unstable families, unemployment, inadequate housing,
physical and sexual abuse, drug and alcohol addiction, poverty
and despair, and involvement in the occult.

### Response 1: Practical assistance

St. Mary's has responded well to the practical needs of individuals, but it has been unable so far to devise adequate structures to provide hope in the community as a whole. A family
support group was started, to offer debt counselling and encouragement for those who wanted to become more self-reliant.
However it was unable to attract the clientele it aimed to serve.
Again, St. Mary's regularly supplies basic furniture and household items to destitute people being rehoused: but only on an ad
hoc basis. It has so far been impossible to establish a permanent
agency to do this work. Nevertheless the parish recognizes that
a more organized and structured response is needed.

### Response 2: A new kind of praying

The new area of mission is creating a new concern for 'spiritual warfare.' St Mary's has never been a charismatic church, in
the accepted meaning of that term. However, there is an increasing awareness in the church that we are struggling *not against
flesh and blood, but against the rulers, against the authorities, against*

*the powers of this dark world and against the spiritual forces of evil in the heavenly realms.* Those who visit the unchurched parts of the parish insist on spending time praying in and for the streets they will visit. They tell their prayer supporters to ask the Lord to protect them, and to hinder and expel their enemy as they go from door to door.

### Response 3: New preaching agenda

At the same time, outreach to unchurched parts of the parish has had an unexpected effect on Bible teaching in the church. This stems from the negative image of the Bible and church among unchurched people. English society thinks it knows about Christianity, whereas it is completely ignorant. Most people take it for granted that the Bible is impossible to understand; and that it is full of contradictions; and in any case it is quite irrelevant to today's world. Whenever outsiders attend St. Mary's services — which is all the time — the preacher must carefully explain the Bible's meaning and relevance for someone who is deeply sceptical.

Our preaching has to begin from the practical concerns of people's lives, as we demonstrate that the Bible contains God's clear commands by which we must live. For example, it comes as an unwelcome shock to some to hear that God demands faithfulness and commitment to a marriage partner: so this simple message must be declared powerfully.

## A Hermeneutic for St. Mary's New Mission

How can St. Mary's claim that its mission is being carried out in submission to the Word of God in Scripture? Has it not been dictated entirely by external circumstances?

Such a question misunderstands the way in which the Word of God shapes mission. Scholars have pointed out that our presuppositions and expectations affect what we find in the Scriptures. Such expectations are influenced by our own history and circumstances. We do not come to the Scriptures with an empty mind, but we already have questions that we want God to answer. Nevertheless, God is not limited by our questions. In reading the Bible, the interpreter must allow his own presuppositions and his own pre-understanding to be modified or even completely reshaped by the text itself... There must be a constant dialogue between the interpreter and the text. The hermeneutical circle is not only unavoidable but desirable.[1]

In other words, Christians do not approach Scripture like hired servants, waiting without interest for today's instructions from their employer. They come as God's sons and daughters, eager to know how to advance the work of the Father's kingdom, to which they are already committed and for which they are already working. We will find that Scripture shapes mission at two levels.

### Scripture shaping mission: at a practical level

At an immediate and practical level, Scripture suggests how a church should respond to the circumstances in which its mission must be carried out.

At every point in St. Mary's mission outlined above, Christians have searched the Scriptures for God's guidance. For example, circumstances have given prominence to lay ministries: so the church has given new attention to what the New Testament teaches about ministry. This has led to new recognition of the gifts and calling of all God's people. Clergy have gladly surrendered any notion that they are a separate caste from the people. They are given their proper role as overseers, teachers, encouragers, and enablers of the people of God.

Again, circumstances have compelled St. Mary's to have a mission among the unchurched; so the church has begun to consider the motives and methods of the apostles' first mission to the unchurched. St. Mary's is glad that others have already done much of the biblical spadework: its study has benefitted from Willow Creek Community Church's insistence on the NT principle that 'Lost people matter to God'. 'Seeker friendly' church services are one immediate result; and two different 'seeker targetted' ventures (one in a new church plant, and the other aimed at young people) are being contemplated. Similarly the church planting movement offers insights on how to put the New Testament mission into a contemporary context. St. Mary's vision of a parish centre surrounded by satellite congregations is the result.

Likewise the new focus on spiritual warfare, and on Bible teaching which addresses issues of practical Christian living, are biblical responses to the new kinds of people St. Mary's mission is meeting. Revd. Chris Boyce, the curate at St. Mary's Centre, finds that he has to concentrate his preaching and pastoral work on explaining what the Bible teaches about obedience to God's commands in marriage and every area of life. The Centre has also adopted an outreach strategy of prayer visiting (calling on unchurched neighbours and inviting them to submit prayer requests for which the whole congregation will pray): a restrained and Anglican form of 'power encounter' evangelism.

### Scripture shaping mission: at a deep level

However the hermeneutical circle of Scripture reading also shapes mission at a deeper level. This deeper level involves the church's fundamental understanding of what the whole message of Scripture is about: how we integrate the doctrines we believe.

No doubt all evangelicals could jot down on an envelope half-a-dozen doctrines or teachings which are of fundamental importance to our faith: the world's creation by God Almighty; the Fall, with its effects; God's plan of salvation, seen first in the promise to Abraham and the choosing of Israel; his coming into the world in the person of Jesus Christ; the redemption won through cross and resurrection; the pouring out of God's Holy Spirit. But even if we agree on these doctrines, there is room for different emphases which emerge from our reading of Scripture.

At a deep level any church has an inbuilt tendency — developed in the dialogue between its history and its reading of the Bible — to identify a theme or themes as of special importance in Scripture. For example in the Church of the Province of Kenya (where I worked for eleven years) the theme of eschatology was of great importance. The Church lived its life and preached in full awareness of God's coming judgment: a judgment which would be seen in the political, economic and social life of the nation, even before the final day when the Lord returns. In its reading of Scripture and in preaching, the church constantly returned to this theme.

Another example: in official circles in the Church of England for some years there has been steady promotion of the theme of joyful worship and celebration. In the Church of England's reading, almost every event in the life of Christ has been taken as a basis for celebration: the joys and tragedies of ordinary life are given new and hopeful meaning by being identified or associated with the life of Christ.

In the 'church culture' of St. Mary's the theme of mission, God's sending of his people out into the world, appears to be dominant. This theme is reflected in St. Mary's intense interest in mission outside its own parish boundaries (it sends support to numerous churches, organizations and individuals in various continents). It emerges in preaching: the congregation is regularly challenged to reach out to our many neighbours in Upton who do not know Jesus, and whose lives are blighted or oppressed. It is the background to a continuous programme of visiting door-to-door in the parish. It is seen in a rhythm of special outreach events in the life of the parish: every five years or so, special programmes of addresses by a visiting speaker are planned.

It is well for a church to recognize its chosen integrating theme in the Bible, and for two reasons: first, so that it can explore its richness more systematically; and second, so that it can admit that its theme may underplay some vital part of the Scripture, and so become attentive to the Holy Spirit when he speaks outside that theme.

## Conclusion: How the Bible shapes our Mission

The Bible shapes our mission in dialogue with the circumstances and realities in which the church lives.

We begin with a deep, foundation-level perception of what is important in Scripture — the themes which integrate our understanding of the Bible. I guess that most of us received our ruling themes from those who first taught us the Christian faith, or from the churches where we are members. These deep perceptions do not easily change. We are wise to be self-aware enough to recognize our own choice of theme, and to admit that a different choice of theme is possible.

When the circumstance of our church's life change, its mission may also change radically: as has happened at St. Mary's in recent years. The new realities send the church back to the Bible to discover what its new mission is. In theory, St. Mary's might have ignored the new realities, held fast to its declining role as an eclectic congregation, and refused the cross-cultural challenges of outreach in its own parish. In practice, St. Mary's interest in the theme of mission compelled it to modify its approach. In this way its response to new circumstances was dictated by the Bible, and not merely by the circumstances themselves.

Finally, the practical details of St. Mary's mission (church planting strategy, lay ministry, holistic concerns, spiritual warfare) are suggested by the church's reading of Bible passages in which God has addressed these very issues. Here too our understanding is worked out in a dialogue between the text of Scripture and ourselves as culture, tradition and history have formed us: but we are confident in the Holy Spirit's ability to guide us by this means into something not too far from what he wants!

## Note

1. G.N. Stanton, "Presuppositions in New Testament Criticism" in I.H. Marshall (ed.), *New Testament Interpretation* (Exeter: Paternoster, 1977).

# Scripture and Mission in an Inner City Area in the UK

*Ida Glaser*

For the evangelical, mission as everything else in life, should be driven by Scripture. But it also works the other way — mission puts us in situations which drive us back to Scripture with urgent questions about ourselves, the people we are sent to and our mission. In this particular case, mission in an inner city community in the UK has driven a study of Genesis 1-11.

The community bears all the marks of deprivation, with high unemployment, divided families, single parents, domestic violence, alcoholism, truancy, and crime rates regularly topping national lists. During the study, civil disturbances reached the international news.

There is a South Asian community, mostly Muslims from rural backgrounds in the Indian sub-continent. There is therefore also racial harassment, some of it violent and even murderous. The local church, with diocesan backing, set up a project to develop relationships with South Asian people, to help the churches to understand them, and to bring the Gospel to them.

The main model chosen for ministry was that of Jesus and the Samaritans — the despised ethnic minority of a related, but different, faith.

- Jesus experienced racism, but refused to react with hostility. His disciples' hostility provoked a statement about his purposes of salvation (Luke 9: 51-6). Therefore we seek to be aware of racism, to fight it, to teach Jesus' intention of saving people from all backgrounds, and to respond with love if people are prejudiced against us.

- Jesus appreciated what was good in the Samaritans — and sometimes they were better than the Jews (Luke 10:25-37, 17:12-18). Therefore we seek to affirm what is good in the Asian cultures and faiths, and sometimes see them as a challenge to ourselves and to our society.

- Jesus brought them the Good News — by breaking barriers and prejudices, and by spending time with one person who took the message back to her community (John 4:1-42). Therefore we seek to share the Gospel patiently as we relate with individuals and families. The pattern of Jesus' conversation encourages us in ministering to women, in accepting their friendship, in understanding their families, and in moving from questions of religion to questions of relationship with God. Most importantly, it encourages us to lavish time on people in ways that might seem wasteful.

In short, we have worked to an incarnational model, being part of the community, seeking to speak the Gospel as we live it and struggling to obey the commandment to "love our neighbours as ourselves."

Questions arise as such a model is put into practice:

**Questions of understanding** — not only of facts about religion and culture, but also of human beings and relationships, and of the effects of Islam on our Muslim neighbours and our reactions to them. Then there are questions about the roots of criminal behaviour and how to deal with it — from the point of view of both victims and criminals.

**Questions of practice** — how do we build relationships, relate to Muslim leaders, support victims of racism, deal with prejudices within the church, support Muslim families under stress, help people relate to British cultures...? And how do we make the Gospel clear to them?

It is to the Scriptures that we turn with our questions; but to which part of Scripture do we turn? And how do we apply it in our particular context?

Because I wanted to look at fundamental issues of understanding the world, I turned to Genesis 1-11. Because I wanted
to understand Muslims, I decided to attempt a comparative
study with the Qur'an. Because Christians and Muslims often
use similar words with different contents, I decided to avoid a
direct study of concepts. Because the Bible and the Qur'an are
such different books, I decided to use stories as common ground.

My method has been to read the Biblical and Qur'anic stories,
trying to listen to the Qur'an from the point of view of some of
the Muslims in our community. I have then asked, "How are the
stories the same, and how are they different?" and used the
answers to address further questions to the texts. I have consciously done this in the context of events in the community and
in my life and ministry.

In what follows, I shall share some of the results of this
process, focussing on some of the differences in the stories that
are relevant to questions concerning family, gender and crime
that arise with urgency in the particular context.

## Differences in the Stories

### Adam and Eve *(mainly Surah 2, Baqara, 30-39 and Genesis 2-3).*

a. The Qur'an uses the picture of vicegerent (khalifa) to describe human beings, whereas the Bible uses "image of God." The
Qur'an says that God taught Adam the names, whereas the Bible
says that Adam was given the job of naming the animals.

b. The Qur'an gives much space to the spiritual powers — a
discussion with the angels over the creation of man, the bowing
of the angels to Adam, and the fall of Satan. The temptation is
attributed to Satan, there being no mention of the snake.

c. The Qur'an has Adam as well as Eve deceived into thinking
that they were not doing wrong in eating the forbidden fruit. The
Bible is clear that Adam was not deceived at all; and it does not
suggest that Eve thought that she was doing right.

d. The Qur'anic Adam repents as soon as he realizes that he
has done wrong. The Biblical Adam denies responsibility, and
we do not know whether he ever repented.

e. The Qur'an has no separate treatment of Eve — Adam's spouse is mentioned but not named, and is only known to be present because of dual verbs. There is no equivalent of the marriage ordinance in Gen. 2:26, and no account of Eve as mother and namer of sons to parallel Genesis 4:1-2.

### Cain and Abel *(Surah 5, Ma'idah, 30-35 and Genesis 4)*

a. The focus of the Qur'anic story is Abel, the innocent victim, with Cain as villain. Genesis focuses on Cain — his struggles and his punishment.

b. In the Qur'an, God does not speak: it is Abel that exhorts his brother. In Genesis, Abel does not speak: most of the story is about God speaking with Cain.

### Noah *(Surah 71, Nuh, Surah 11, Hud, 36-48 etc. and Genesis 6-9).*

a. In the Qur'an, Noah is primarily a prophet to his people, and the judgment comes because they reject him and his message. In the Bible, he is simply a righteous man (albeit by grace), and the people are destroyed because of moral wickedness.

c. In the Bible, the covenant to save Noah includes his family (6:18). In the Qur'an, it is not family but believers who are saved, and Noah's wife and one of his sons are excluded.

### Babel *(Surah 16, Nahl, 26 and Genesis 11:1-12).*

There is only one verse in the Qur'an that probably refers to Babel, but there are Muslim stories about it. As in some Jewish comment, they have the tower built up to attack God. The Bible does not actually say this: it sees the confusion of the languages not so much as a punishment for what has been done as a preventative measure against what might be done. Thus the tower in the Qur'anic story falls on the people's heads and kills them, while in Genesis they are not destroyed but confused and scattered.

### Genealogies

The whole structure of Genesis 1:11 is built around the genealogies and the table of nations. There is no parallel in the Qur'an, the context for Muhammed's prophethood being given in terms of lists of prophets rather than lists of ancestors.

## Implications

### Family and community

The importance of family and community is mainly seen in the genealogical structure of the Genesis passages. Then there is the build-up of human society from the husband-wife relationship through siblings to families, communities and nations. In particular, the Noah story focuses on family. The Qur'anic account may seem to be, as Muslims claim, more "moral" in who is saved and who is judged, but it throws the Biblical picture of family solidarity into relief and underlines its importance as the basis of the human race. The whole family belongs together, even though some members may be less than satisfactory. Even blessings and cursings go in families.

The table of nations then focuses on communities, but even here they are *related* communities. Sometimes, it is difficult to distinguish between families and nations. This leads on to the establishment of covenant with Abraham and his *family*.

These insights are important in our context:

They contribute to the diagnosis of problems, especially those resulting from lack of family cohesion in the white community. Among the Muslims, family identity is usually strong, but cultural and communal identity may be confused, especially for second and third generation immigrants.

They put nations and languages into perspective, first by implying that they are part of God's blessing and providence as the remade world is replenished in Genesis 10, and then by showing that misunderstanding and scattering is part of God's judgment on and limitation of sin.

They provide a corrective to individualistic western thinking, and affirm Muslim views of the importance of family. However, they also provide a corrective to over-emphasis on the family within the Muslim community, by pointing out the sins and tensions within groups.

One of the most important implications of the way that Genesis so carefully places people in their families, communities, nations and territories is simply that these locations are important. As members of the Kingdom and Family of God, we still need to know where we belong in the human areas. Even Jesus knew where he belonged according to his human descent as well as according to his divine origin (Matthew 1). The corollary of this is that, when people lose their sense of location, things go wrong. This is why Cain's punishment was so terrible, and it is evident in all sectors of our community.

### Male and female

Male-female relationships are among the most problematic aspects of both white and Asian communities. The white community needs to take notice of the marriage ordinances and the role of parents. It also needs to work on understanding male-female dynamics in Muslim society.

As a woman, I also see much need for re-assessment in this area for Muslim families. Although marriage bonds are strong, the position of women within them is often very difficult. The Genesis passages offer some help:

The matriarchal marriage institution points out the husband's position in marriage, particularly the breaking of bonding with his mother. In the Muslim communities, the mother-son bond is one of the strongest. The daughter-in-law comes to live in the husband's home, and is definitely second to his mother. Genesis affirms the importance of the mother, as it describes Eve as mother and shows her naming her sons. However, it cautions against carrying the bonding beyond marriage.

Within many Muslim marriages, roles are very clearly defined, and wives may be considered to have responsibility for their husbands' as well as their children's behaviour. If things go wrong, it is generally seen as the woman's fault — even if she is being beaten by her husband, she is blamed. Genesis 3 helps us to see this in the context of a basic human tendency to shift responsibility. Of course, Muslim women as well as Muslim men have this tendency, but this is on an individual level whereas the men's shifting is part of the system.

Perhaps the most important implication of the Genesis passages is that male-female relationships have gone fundamentally wrong. Both God's words to the woman and the discussion in the garden show that the original balance of roles and mutuality of responsibility have been upset. The lack of a doctrine of fall in Islam implies a denial of this: that there is enmity between humans and Satan following the experience of Adam and Eve, but no fundamental imbalance in gender roles. This can result in imbalance being considered natural rather than wrong.

### Crime and punishment

The roots of violent crime as seen in Genesis 4 include jealousy and vengeance. Chapter 6 adds lust, wickedness of heart, and the overthrowing of God's ordering of his creation. This takes us further into the question of sin and responsibility.

Genesis stresses the accountability of humankind, deliberate rebellion against God, and the implication of groups in the sins of their members. The Qur'anic Adam stories emphasize the role of the devil and see the basic human problem as ignorance and deception rather than rebellion. On the other hand, the Cain and Abel story has Cain as thoroughly wicked compared to his brother who is thoroughly good. The Noah story, too, divides mankind into the good, who accept the prophet, and the bad, who reject him.

One of the most hopeful aspects of these stories — both Biblical and Qur'anic — for victims of crime and harassment in our inner city area is the assurance that God will judge. The police and other authorities might be inefficient or ineffective, but in the end God will put it all right.

However, Genesis shows that God is also on the side of the criminals. In the case of the worst, Cain the fratricide, God does not only listen to the cry of the blood of the innocent victim: He also listens to the guilty murderer, and ameliorates the punishment.

## So What?

### An analysis of our inner city problems

Loss of location; imbalance in gender roles, particularly in the context of marriage; jealousy, lust and ambition — Asian and western groups are affected by these in different ways, but the fundamental areas of tension are the same. This is perhaps because they are symptoms of the underlying rebellion and denial of responsibility that are common to all humankind.

### An analysis that differs from that of Islam

The fundamental differences in notions of potential relationships between humans and God that are hinted at in the "vicegerent"/"image of God" difference, and in the role of Adam in the naming, work out in different ideas about human responsibility and need. There are various strands in Islamic thinking about this, but two stand out from these stories:

Mankind's fundamental problems are deception and forgetfulness: what we need is reminder and information.

The world is divided into believers and unbelievers, good and bad — although it is possible for people to move from one sphere to the other.

### God's mission

God's response to His world gone wrong is not mainly, as in the Qur'anic picture, the sending of prophets, the destruction of the wicked and the saving of the good.

God judges, but he chooses to limit his judgment — Adam and Eve do not die physically immediately, Cain is only exiled and receives his mark, Noah and his family are saved, and the generation of Babel is scattered but not destroyed.

God chooses never to destroy totally. He commits Himself to working with the people he has made. In that the flood is unique, God will never again start from scratch. We are all under the Noahic covenant.

God saves whoever he chooses. Why was Abel's sacrifice acceptable? Was Noah the only righteous man? What was his righteousness, and how did it relate to God's grace? Why was his family saved with him?

While God is scrupulously just in his judgments, salvation is by God's grace and through his chosen means. The scandal of particularity is not in who is condemned, but in who is saved.

Salvation through the family of Abraham is for all. The peoples of the earth described in Genesis 1-11 are the peoples to be blessed through Abraham, and therefore through Jesus Christ (Gen. 12:3, Eph. 3:6).

## Pointers for our mission

*The pointer of our common humanity.* We should relate to our Muslim neighbours as to anyone else — as human beings created and loved by God, and saved from destruction under the Noahic covenant. We should recognize our common needs, and the common purposes for which God created us. In practice, this implies sufficient understanding of, and sometimes laying aside of, culture to lay bare our common natures.

*The pointer of our common predicament.* This is not only a common fallenness, but a sharing in the inner city environment, and in problems of dis-location and family tensions. In practice, it implies sharing experiences, listening to pain and becoming involved in attempts at amelioration.

*The need to present a correct analysis of that predicament.* Given that the Bible starts with Genesis 1-11 and that the first function of the Holy Spirit is to convince the world of sin (John 16:8), this need is a starting point. It informs and drives not only our conversation, but also our responses to difficult situations and particularly to children.

*The need to affirm peoples' locations.* We seek to accept and affirm our own backgrounds, and encourage Muslim people to appreciate theirs. This does not mean that we ignore wrong aspects of culture, but that we face them rather than denying them. This is particularly important:

- for Christian people, in the light of current tendencies to feel ashamed of western imperialism, secular culture and white racism.
- for the younger generations of Muslims who are tempted to jettison either their Asian background or their western context.

*The need to let God be judge.* This is important:

- in our responses to the criminal sub-culture, especially in view of a tendency amongst Muslims to label whole groups of people as "bad." Although we seek to cause no unnecessary offence or misunderstanding by our lifestyles, we sometimes need to make the same point that Jesus did when He went openly to eat with tax-collectors and sinners.

- in our expectations of what kind of responses to Islam, to the Gospel and to ourselves God might find satisfactory.

*The purpose of the covenant people.* As the choice of Abraham leaves no room for self-congratulation on the part of the Jews (cf Deut. 7:7), so the fact of our being followers of Jesus Christ leaves us no room for pride. However, as the call of Abraham shows that God's purpose was not only for his family but for all families, so his purpose in calling us to Christ is that others should also receive the blessing that he came to bring. We need to tell people about Jesus as well as working out our shared humanity and predicament. We need to communicate the answers as well as the analysis, and to offer the most important and secure location as children of the Heavenly Father.

It is striking that these pointers for mission are consistent with those derived from the "Jesus and the Samaritan" model. That is, they affirm the ways in which we are already working, and help us to develop them. That leaves us with some interesting, if uncomfortable, questions:

- Would a different model as context have given rise to a different understanding of Genesis 1-11? Have I simply read my own ministry into the study?
- Would a different biblical passage have challenged us to change the original model?
- Or is it that Jesus incarnates God's own response to Genesis 1-11, and that our attempts at ministry, although stumbling, are consistent with His?

# Little Trinity Anglican Church, Toronto, Canada

*Peter C. Moore*

**Our mission**

Our mission is to uphold classical Christian norms for sexual behaviour in church and society in the face of vigorous challenges to it from homosexual activists and sympathizers.

Steered our way by a friend at work, George began attending Little Trinity Church on a fairly regular basis. Since our fellowship contains many singles of both sexes, he did not stand out in any way. However, while appearing to melt into the woodwork, George was actually watching and listening with growing interest.

George had been an active member of Toronto's sizeable gay community since he had come to accept his homosexual orientation at the age of 25. Although he had managed to keep his secret from many straight friends, he had been involved in a number of relationships with men. One man to whom George was attracted turned out to be a Christian, and suggested he read *Mere Christianity*. This proved to be a turning point which led George to the realization that he needed to break off his current relationship and own up to someone he could trust.

As George's rector I was the one to whom he turned. I had guessed his orientation, but over lunch in the quiet corner of a restaurant I let him come out to me and share his life's story. I later learned that this was a watershed experience, and that my

acceptance of him reaffirmed the acceptance that he was beginning to feel from Jesus Christ. I told him that he would have to
leave the gay lifestyle, and directed him to an organization in
town that was supporting gays who wanted help in changing
their behaviour and orientation. I assured him that changing his
sexual orientation would involve a long and arduous path.

The New Directions organization I referred him to immediately paired him with another former homosexual and through
that relationship George began to gain perspective on his life,
and in a halting way to redirect his thinking. Meanwhile George
was becoming more active at our Church. He began reading
Scripture and taking communion regularly, and joined one of
our small fellowship groups for weekly Bible study and prayer.
His heart was strongly responding to the Gospel.

Believing that he must tell one or two other people who could
hold him accountable in his struggle, George came out to a
couple to others — one being a divorced woman with whom he
subsequently fell in love and who is now his wife. While he says
he still has homosexual desires, George's marriage (now almost
two years old) seems solid, and he is growing as a Christian by
leaps and bounds. He currently serves as chairman of one of our
Church's ministries, and writes: "My homosexuality is further
and further behind me every day... Sometimes I felt like I would
never get ahead of it and that I would never become straight. But
I am, it feels great, and it is comforting to *know* that I am obeying
God and living a life which is in alignment with His plan for me."

## Our Church

Little Trinity is not a church where homosexuals would auto-
matically assume they might find a welcome. Prior to my arrival
as a rector just over seven years ago, an organist who had refused
to break off a homosexual relationship had been asked to leave.
While reasons other than his sexual behaviour were given for the
dismissal, virtually everyone knew that there were other factors
involved. Little Trinity had a long and well-established reputation of upholding orthodox evangelical doctrine and classical
Christian norms.

A gathered church which worships downtown in the city's

oldest surviving church building, "Little T" here has maintained a low-church evangelical witness for virtually all of its 150-year history. It is closely allied to Wycliffe College, an evangelical Anglican theological college in Toronto, and is composed of a highly educated group of professionals many of whom have Inter-Varsity Christian Fellowship roots. It has a budget in excess of $400,000, a pastoral staff of three, supports 22 "koinonia" groups involving over a half of the active membership, and has a historical commitment to missions.

## Our City

Toronto over the past 25 years has become a "world class" city with a highly developed cultural life, a cosmopolitan citizenship, and (I can't resist) a World Series championship baseball team! Located just outside our parish boundaries is the heart of Toronto's homosexual community.

Homosexuality has become an important issue in this city. Being the film capital of Canada, Toronto draws many people who have liberal views on sexual behaviour. The old "Upper Canada" conservative hegemony has been replaced by a left-leaning city government and media elite who have pushed the boundaries of acceptable behaviour outwards. Gay Pride Day is a big event. The City's Board of Education has pushed through a pro-gay curriculum for secondary school students which argues that homosexual behaviour is the moral equivalent of heterosexual marriage. Brochures with graphic illustrations of homosexual activity are printed by agencies affiliated with the city government for distribution to school children and teens. Despite a serious recession, hundreds of thousands of taxpayer dollars are donated by the Province to gay civic groups which produce dramatic productions involving, for example, "hands-on sado-masochistic dramatizations."

Nationally, homosexuals have won the right to serve in Canada's military forces, and increasingly "sexual orientation" is interpreted by the courts as one of the areas deserving of special protection under the Charter of Rights and Freedoms. The church is increasingly on the defensive, and pressures to conform to the prevailing cultural viewpoint are strong. For example, the country's largest Protestant denomination, the United Church, has now disbarred exclusion of noncelibate homosexuals from the ordained ministry. Despite the fact that this has caused at least 20,000 members and many congregations to leave the United Church, active lobby groups like Integrity in the Anglican Church are committed to gaining the same rights within other denominations.

## Our Awakening

Although I had read around the subject of homosexuality for years and had formed my own convictions, my own awakening to the serious nature of the contemporary challenge came in 1991, whilst reading a book by a United Church minister about the homosexual agenda. The congregation's awakening stemmed from an incident in the Diocese of Toronto which hit the world press. The rector of a major parish had come out about his homosexuality to a few parishioners, including some in leadership. Realizing that the information was not containable and was quickly producing a parish crisis, he went to our bishop, fully expecting the bishop's known "gay positive" attitude to weigh in his favour. To his surprise the bishop, citing a 1969 bishops' guideline rejecting the ordination of homosexuals who were unwilling to remain celibate, took a firm line. The gay minister refused the bishop's counsel that he give up his current relationship with a man, was promptly relieved of his duties as rector and inhibited from functioning as a priest. The minister decided to fight, launching a $500,000 lawsuit against the bishop for wrongful dismissal and asking for a bishop's court to hear the case. TIME magazine, the *New York Times,* as well as several major TV networks carried bits and pieces of the story. Bishop Spong of New Jersey, a noted supporter of homosexual ordination, flew to Toronto to testify in his defence. While the court (as was expected) decided in the bishop's favour, the case is far from over. The gay minister has written a book entitled *In the Courts of the Lord,* and a made-for-TV movie is on the way. Meanwhile, during the proceedings of the bishop's court it was revealed that the Primate of the Anglican Church of Canada knowingly ordained a practising homosexual, and General Synod has instructed the entire church to continue to study the issue until —

as one bishop cynically says — conservatives in the Church come around or give up the fight.

## Our Biblical Foundations

Undergirding our approach to this whole issue is a firm belief in the authority of the Bible and its clarity on this issue. This latter point has had to be made in the light of many attempts by liberal theologians to discredit the historic understanding of Scripture on homosexuality.

Our assumption is that in the light of Genesis 2 homosexuality is a disorder in the sexual life, and like all disorders is partially reversible in this life through the redeeming power of God and fully reversible in the life to come.

We reject the facile efforts to interpret the sin of Sodom solely as a breach of hospitality, the Levitical holiness codes as dealing primarily with ritual (rather than moral) impurity, the references of St. Paul in Romans as one referring only to "perverts" (heterosexuals acting homosexually) rather than "inverts" (homosexuals acting according to their natures), or as referring mainly to homosexual prostitution rather than consensual gay sex.

We are saddened by the efforts to portray David, Jonathan, Paul, Timothy and even Jesus as latent or overt homosexuals, and recognize the sinister hand of our Enemy in all attempts to popularize such views. We find the Bible's repugnance towards homosexuality to be rooted in its high view of heterosexual monogamy which according to Genesis 1:27 and 2:24 is part of the Creator's plan whereby we discover what it is to be fully human.

Behind the various attempts to distort the Bible's teaching on homosexuality lie faulty hermeneutical principles which then lead to easily discreditable positions. These arise from a failure to insist that the Old Testament be interpreted by the New, that Jesus (whose silence on homosexuality is sometimes taken as implicit endorsement) be interpreted by Paul, and that narrative portions (like David and Jonathan) be interpreted by ethical ones.

Moreover, we are troubled by the fact that among leading biblical theologians and ethicists there is a widespread assault on the idea that the Bible contains timeless norms which can be applied to cultural situations removed from their original context. We agree with Professor O'Donovan who asks: "If [Mosaic sayings] are irrelevant because [they are] context-dependent, [wouldn't it] follow that anything said by anybody in the past is irrelevant for the same reasons?" (See my article "Getting to the heart of the debate on ethics" in the appendix.)

We are grateful for the many who have written clearly on this subject from the perspective of a high view of Scripture, including a number of Anglican Evangelicals: John Stott, Oliver O'Donovan, David Atkinson, and John W. Howe. We are grateful for those who, although not identified specifically with the evangelical wing of the church, nonetheless have many fine things to say on this issue: David Scott, Philip Turner, Richard Hays, Elizabeth Moberly, Helmut Thielicke, and the bishops of the Church of England whose "Issues in Human Sexuality" (1991) brings a great deal of light to the subject. *A Wholesome Example* is an excellent manuscript on homosexuality written by Episcopalians on the Virginia Theological Seminary faculty.

## Our Strategy

Because we needed to respond to a multi-pronged attack we were aware that we should not rely on just one approach. Therefore, with the support of our Churchwardens and Council, we have moved forward on many fronts.

### *Support*

We support several parishioners who have identified themselves as having problems with homosexual temptations, and have been pastorally available to them on a one-to-one basis. Some are living chaste lives, others have fallen occasionally into sexual sin, and one case involves a brother who has multiple problems and who has as yet to see his problem as sin. We have also invited a local ministry aimed at the homosexual community to run day-long conferences at Little Trinity, and have offered office space to assist them in their ministry to AIDS victims.

### *Education*

This has been our strongest approach. I have written articles and book reviews for national magazines on this subject. I have created a video on "The Bible and homosexuality" which has been distributed by Episcopalians United, a conservative lobby group in the States, and been seen by approximately 3000 people. I have appeared on national TV with the above mentioned gay minister, taking the other side. I have spoken at many conferences on issues related to sexuality, and have spoken on the floor of our Diocesan Synod defending the Biblical view of homosexuality. A major Anglican Evangelical conference, Essentials '94, modelled on the NEAC congresses, will provide a further opportunity for education on this issue, and I shall be speaking on the issue of sexuality there.

Early in my ministry here, before sexuality issues gained national prominence, I realized that as a parish we needed to be united in our thinking. Therefore, taking advantage of Oliver O'Donovan's sabbatical here, and drawing on the experiences of a Christian psychiatrist in the parish plus a former lesbian who was engaged in a ministry to gays, we organized an adult education event on a "Biblical and Pastoral Approach to Homosexuality." The talks given were edited and became the basis of a book on homosexuality geared to Canadian churches: *A Crisis of Understanding* (1988). Subsequent adult education events at Little Trinity have sought to keep the congregation current on this subject.

Finally, we produced an annotated bibliography on Christianity and homosexuality which has been made available to interested persons.

### Networking

Painfully aware of the fear of speaking out which many who share orthodox views on this subject have, we have begun to network among the clergy and the community.

My assistant was invited to join the Bishop's Task Force on Homosexuality which will soon present a report on its findings. As one of the three orthodox voices on this important committee, he has worked hard to present a balanced biblical viewpoint. In part because of his involvement the Bishop has begun turning to our parish to recommend conservative spokespeople on homosexuality for events like the upcoming House of Bishops meeting. Thankfully also, George, whose story introduced this paper, was willing to join the Task Force as a laymember, and his story will be included in the final report.

We formed a clergy study group on homosexuality, intentionally drawing together clergy from a variety of churchmanship and theological backgrounds. This group met several times, produced a thoughtful report, and is now meeting with a small group of bishops to assist them in their struggle within the House of Bishops where pro-gay sentiment seems quite strong.

We have encouraged one of our young people to become a youth delegate to Synod where she has borne witness to her biblical views among other youth delegates who decidedly do not share them. And one of our former Wardens, an articulate lawyer, stood for election to the Diocese Executive Council. He, together with another graduate student, is also preparing a major paper on a biblical, theological, and pastoral approach to homosexuality which will be endorsed by our entire parish Council and sent to Toronto's College of Bishops.

### *Protest*

Confronting the powers sometimes takes the form of open protest. Since Ontario's socialist government has taken an open stand for "homosexual rights," activists have sought to advance the gay agenda on a variety of fronts. The City of Toronto's Board of Education has produced an unacceptable curriculum for use in schools despite the protests of parent groups. It portrays homosexual activity as morally neutral, holds traditional religious scruples up for ridicule, provides pro-gay spokespeople for classroom discussion while refusing anti-gay spokespeople, and through a city-funded counselling service recommends teens who are troubled by their sexual identity to see various pro-gay organizations for counsel. One such organization, mentioned in the original document, openly advocates "safe sado-masochistic sex practices."

Little Trinity helped create a parents' task force to investigate the Board of Education, and with the support of a few Board members who are appalled at their colleagues' actions, has become involved in direct protest: demonstrations in front of the Board's offices, publicized seminars, a literature campaign, letter writing to elected officials, radio and TV talk shows to "present the other side." Plans are also being laid to assist the election campaigns of those who run against targetted Board members.

All of this has stirred many otherwise reticent people into action. For instance, a noted linguistic anthropologist in our parish has taken to writing letters of commendation and criticism to major TV networks for their biased or (occasionally) fair reportage on this issue. Several laypeople have emerged as gifted spokespeople for biblical ethics, addressing groups of hundreds and, through radio and TV, even thousands of people.

## Our Paradigm

It would be wrong to assume that all this activity is motivated by our reading of a few texts in the Old and New Testament. Our paradigm is our Lord himself. We see him dealing with the woman taken in adultery in John 8. Pressed to condemn her by the righteous, he found himself caught between the plain teaching of the Mosaic law and his own understanding of the character of God. How to reconcile the two?

Jesus chose a pastoral approach to the woman, not condemning her but setting her free to live a new life in grateful response to his acceptance. Similarly, we aim to treat homosexual people with no less sensitivity and grace.

However, those convinced of the rightness of their cause, who are willing to use this fallen woman to advance their own power base as arbiters of official policy, he treated confrontationally. He exposed their hypocrisy and forced them to think more deeply about the nature of sin. By turning the spotlight away from the woman and onto their own lusts, he upheld the law of God and effectively silenced them at the same time.

# The Use of Scripture in the Iglesia Anglicana de Chile

*Alfredo Cooper*

## Background and Context

The Iglesia Anglicana de Chile (IACH) is a fruit of British Mission endeavour. The particular missionaries who planted the first Chilean Anglican churches were mostly (though not exclusively) of a conservative evangelical persuasion. Nurtured in the mission fervour of mid-19th century England, Captain Allen Gardiner and the first SAMS missionaries who sought to reach the indigenous peoples of Tierra del Fuego were clearly inspired in the great Scriptural mandates: the Great Commission and the Great Commandment. Theirs was a mission of evangelism and of mercy. Together with baptizing the Chagan, Ona, Araucano indigenous peoples, they brought them schools, hospitals, and agricultural expertise. Later mission policy developed by SAMS and the emerging national church, throughout the Southern Cone always kept to this understanding of biblical principles of Mission.

During the last twenty years, with the emergence of national leadership, policy and planning have increasingly been shouldered by the Latin American church. In the past the conservative evangelical norm was accepted *ipso facto* in the IACH as a heritage from the missionary founders to be preserved unquestioned. Now, political, social, economic factors faced by the national church during the upheavals of the '70s and '80s have forced a renewed "Chilean" reflection on Scripture. Further, the

IACH had decided on an evangelistic move into the cities during the '60s. Resultant conversion growth brought people with a higher social and educational status to the church. The previously simple Anglican churches of the deep rural South now began to meet with university graduates and businessmen, politicians and doctors as brethren at national conferences. An urgent demand for national clergy trained to a level compatible with the new requirements of the growing city churches led to programmes of theological training (mostly by extension). Interestingly, the resulting theological reflection and church growth dynamics have tended to strengthen that previously held adherence to Scripture. In some areas (participation of children at Communion, development of new evangelistic methods, extension theological training, lay leadership and mobilization), the emerging national thinking has dared to implement modern and fruitful applications of the cherished Scriptural principle.

## Our Worship seeks to be Biblical

Today the Anglican church in Chile is comprised of close to 90 congregations, pastored by 35 clergy. Although the transculturalised version of the Book of Common Prayer turned out rather severe and European in its format, it has served to maintain worship along the age old Anglican tracks. *Confession, Creeds, Collect, Prayers, Lectionary* as well as various liturgical options for services are all in the book, and these have maintained to a large extent, a healthy balance to worship. Yet Anglican worship is not as attractive, it seems, to the average Chilean, as is Pentecostalism. Simple statistics tell the tale of how 20 percent of Chileans have flocked to the Pentecostal churches during this century, mostly passing by the "safe and sound" Anglicans. This would be true of most places except at the two extremes of the social scale: the Indian congregations and the upper middle classes. In both these areas the biblical principle of worship is expressed in a culturally adapted way and the church in these areas has seen the fruit of this.

The rural Indian work is the oldest and also the most "nationalized." Among the Mapuche churches a simple, biblical Anglicanism is practised. Written liturgical formats are used but usually primacy is given to a free style of worship. The services are simple and often incorporate Indian language and particularities. A new Mapuche Communion Service has been devised. A natural gravity alternates with vigorous manifestations of the supernatural (a dimension which these "people of the earth" are far more familiar with than the city dweller). A visiting English clergyman sat through an hour of singing, another half hour of Indian folk dance in the Spirit, a period when the prophetesses got up and prophesied, lunch, more worship, a long sermon, before he finally sighed "Imagine this in Westminster Abbey!"

## *Pentecostal Anglican*

The reason for this curious mixture of the ancient and the modern, the folk and the liturgical, the charismatic and the sombre, can be traced to the Pentecostal revivals in Chile. Since 1909 an outburst of indigenous Methodism spread all over the modest and poor sectors of the urban shanties penetrating later into the "Anglican held" territories in the South. Our own churches were at times swept into revival outpourings. The typical debate relating to worship style, gifts of the Spirit, abuses and freedom often ensued. The results, however, have been healthy. A natural evangelistic zeal sends Indian evangelists over hill and dale preaching the Gospel, and healing the sick. A high priority on prayer takes the churches into all night vigils and seasons of prayer that again bring refreshing renewals from Heaven. The value of corporate leadership has been appreciated and developed in most of the churches. In all this the Scriptures play a central role, more in a devotional pietistic way than in a studied rationalized mode. This seems to be the more easily absorbed relationship to Scripture that Pentecostalism produces. It would be a mistake to assume that these "Pentecostal type" of Anglicans do not know their Bibles. Quite to the contrary, Scripture can be seen to play a vital role in the building of personal, family, social and church relationships. Where for instance the Minguacos (a traditional Araucano community service project) leads to drunkenness and carousing, the Christians hold Minguacos where after the building of a neighbour's ruca home they will hold a hymn singing Bible study followed by a roast cum Communion Service.

## Mink and Mercedes

Then there is the Anglican church in the upper middle classes the "Mink and Mercedes" set as it has been called. Again the foundations have been a biblical concept of worship, shaped by the liturgies though adapted to the more serious, intellectual, professional culture of European Chile. Work in Santiago began in the '70s and early house churches soon grew to become two medium sized congregations, one of which will plant a third during this year. Whereas Pentecostal evangelism is inherently "anti-Catholic" (in part due to the persecution the early movement received) this sector of the populace is "culturally" anti-Pentecostal. Anglicanism with its faithfulness to liturgy and its more "thinking" approach to Scripture and Religion, attracts. Where Roman Catholicism has made enemies or fails to meet the longing for a more direct relationship to God, the IACH has increasingly provided the alternative. Often asked what the difference between the two churches is, our stock reply has become "Well, the Anglican church is the reformed Catholic church, based on the Bible. Everything that we see the Bible demands, we demand. What is not there we do not require as a mandate for faith or practice." The frantic modern life style that prosperity is bringing to Chile also requires the church to lay on a modern programme. Services must truly bring modern people into a relationship with God. Perhaps not surprisingly in an increasingly hedonistic age, this will often be through an "experience" of God. We understand the Scriptural mandate to know God as a close relationship with him. Again in a prayerful, serious, charismatic style of worship and life, the modern professional Chilean seems to relax and be renewed. Fast conversion growth over the last eight years seems to show that culturally relevant worship is in place.

It is in these sectors of Chilean Anglicanism that some liturgical experiments have been pioneered. Children coming to Communion with their parents, lay participation in the administration of Communion, reflect an emphasis on the family and the laity that is part of these churches. We are interested in developing a limited form of lay presidency at Holy Communion, so that in the absence of a presbyter, the bishop can authorize, after getting the assent of the local church, a lay preacher or suitable lay person to celebrate. A very relaxed, noisy and child filled family atmosphere in the first part of the worship express the Latin community and family spirit. Biblical teaching on the family from pulpit and in the discipling groups are paramount in our church year programme.

It is here too that new approaches to evangelism have been developed.

## Our Evangelism seeks to be Biblical

"Chile para Cristo" is the Pentecostal battle cry as they invade whole communities with Gospel preaching and discipling. Anglicans share this biblical vision of reaching "everyone" with the Gospel, whole neighbourhoods, cities, cultures, nations for Christ. The IACH has not had to respond to the Decade of Evangelism by "adopting" evangelism uncomfortably, rather by refining and adapting the evangelism practised. Conferences for evangelists have uncovered and polished up the gift and ministry of the evangelist, seeking to bring evangelists in from the individualistic lunatic fringe to being part of the local church. Local churches have looked at their communal life style and asked whether everything they "say and do" is Good News. A "life style of evangelism" is being developed in local churches with programmes helping to train and provide opportunity for the more natural person to person witness that "appears" so spontaneously in the Latin American church. In this Scripture has been the reference point as new life has grown. Studies offered at Diocesan Diploma level have reflected again on Evangelism and Mission. As an expression of our serious commitment to the Decade of Evangelism, the IACH joined with other churches of the Province of the Southern Cone in a Mission to Spain during 1992. Over a two month period a church was planted as a result, in Móstoles, in collaboration with the Iglesia Española Reformada Episcopal (Anglican Communion).

After working through many traditional methods of evangelism (open air, door to door, crusades, etc.) a need was sensed in the middle class Barrio Alto churches to adapt outreach to a more "seeker friendly" style. Never have we doubted our duty to "reach the lost" and "share the Gospel with every creature." As we looked at Scripture and as the life of the church developed we noticed how "natural" evangelism in the New Testament seemed. We began to experience several New Testament principles in a surprising way. "New believers bring new believers" has become a fundamental maxim among us. As a new member joined us we would often notice a spiritual rebirth take place. This often took the form of a loving attitude in the home, in the work or study place and to closer everyday relations with people. Often there was an immediate tendency to want to take those acquaintances and relatives to church. So we set about devising programmes whereby new members could feel comfortable about bringing new seekers. A marriage encounter (ME) programme, specially adapted to seekers has met the need. Very often our church is crowded with applicants we have never seen before, eager to experience a ME weekend, encouraged by those who recently went on one and found Christ and love. If even a small percentage of those who attend a ME come to personal faith in Christ, then next Sunday very often six or seven new families walk over the church threshold, each later eager to bring friends and family. A veritable snowballing of new members continue to arrive in this way. The biblical norm "God added daily to the church those that were being saved" is now understood among us.

This natural movement, this divine addition to the church has necessitated a biblical approach to discipling.

## Our Discipling seeks to be Biblical

The IACH has always looked to Scripture for an understanding of what a true Christian disciple is. It has sometimes taken live issues within the local social context to widen that understanding. The desire to live out a relevant, modern expression of the New Testament church has been keenly felt in Latin American evangelical churches. Among Christian university students, the Marxist analysis of society led to much questioning of inherited "Northern" interpretations of Scripture. Liberation theology was an attempt to answer "from below" from the bases of need and injustice that were particularly Latin American, the issues that cried out in frustration before a selfish and narrow pietism. Humanity needed to be saved integrally and not just "spiritually." The Kingdom of God in all its wider implications of humanity living in God's will were worked out quite radically, in both Catholic and Protestant churches. While the IACH has not officially espoused the more extreme forms of Liberation Theology, it has been helped to understand biblical implications of social justice previously unseen in the Scriptural text. The Old Testament prophets, and Christ's own teaching in the Sermon on the Mount and elsewhere challenged us that love in action will often take the church to social and political commitments that may be just as "spiritual" as an evangelistic crusade. In the divided political scenario of '70s and '80s Chile, the IACH sought to implement a ministry of reconciliation. Work was carried out among political prisoners as much as among the Pinochetistas. On the fateful date for the Referendum that finally ousted Pinochet from power, our local church held a Communion Service that symbolized our commitment to a loyalty above that of political faction, to Christ the Lord Himself. During the Service those who were going to vote "No" were asked to hug those who would vote "Yes" and vice versa. We thus hoped to live out in our own church community prophetically hope and healing for Chile, basing ourselves on the biblical principle of reconciliation. Subsequent events in our politics bore us out.

In the local church discipling is seen as being taught to live out the new adopted life style of the Kingdom of God, empowered internally in each believer by the Holy Spirit. A Beginners Group will very often be the way into this new life style that looks to the Scripture for its norm and to the Holy Spirit for its outworking in the modern context.

### Our Lay Mobilization and Leadership Training seek to be Biblical

We have no residential Bible Colleges. Our local churches have, of necessity become our Bible Colleges. It was in these fields that the first attempts at what today is a revolution, Theological Education by Extension, were developed. The SEAN programme, developed by Anglican missionaries in the Southern Cone, today ministers to thousands of students of various denominations, nationalities, languages, all around the world. It was natural that this type of programme should develop here due to the great stock placed on lay leadership. Mobilizing the laity is a key for the future of our work. The Football Trainer concept rather than the One Man Band style of leadership emerged for us in our understanding of early church dynamics. Leaders are there to train the members, who in turn do the ministry, become trained as leaders and train others. 2 Timothy 2:2 is for us more a survival tactic than a theory of discipleship. Lay training programmes using SEAN-TEE materials are thus part of our local church life. In one middle class church a six-year training and mobilizing programme has produced more than eighty leaders in eight years. Some of these are now planting new churches. Our necessity led to the discovery of the effectiveness of the biblical workforce, the laity, every-member ministry. Further extension programmes of theological training develop those with higher possibilities of study.

## Conclusion

It is thus in the outworked life of the young national church that the IACH has rediscovered Scripture for herself. It now behoves the new national leadership to ensure that it is Scripture that continues to provide the bedrock of belief and practice for the challenges of the coming century in the IACH.